THE
SOCIAL & POLITICAL IDEAS OF SOME GREAT THINKERS OF THE RENAISSANCE AND THE REFORMATION

THE
SOCIAL & POLITICAL IDEAS
OF SOME GREAT THINKERS
OF THE RENAISSANCE AND
THE REFORMATION

A SERIES OF LECTURES DELIVERED AT
KING'S COLLEGE UNIVERSITY OF LONDON

EDITED BY

F. J. C. HEARNSHAW M.A. LL.D.

PROFESSOR OF MEDIÆVAL HISTORY IN THE
UNIVERSITY OF LONDON

WITH A PREFACE BY

ERNEST BARKER M.A. D.Litt. LL.D.

PRINCIPAL OF KING'S COLLEGE UNIVERSITY
OF LONDON

BARNES & NOBLE, INC., NEW YORK

PUBLISHERS • BOOKSELLERS • SINCE 1873

First published 1925
by GEORGE G. HARRAP & CO. LTD.
Facsimile reprint 1967
BARNES & NOBLE, INC.
New York, N.Y., 10003

PRINTED IN GREAT BRITAIN
BY PHOTOLITHOGRAPHY
UNWIN BROTHERS LIMITED
WOKING AND LONDON

PREFACE

THE public lectures which, largely under the inspiration and by the efforts of Professor Hearnshaw in the Faculty of Arts and Professor Dendy in the Faculty of Natural Science, have been given for many years past in King's College have already issued in the publication of four volumes based upon courses delivered in the College to general audiences. Professor Dendy, whose sudden death is a serious loss alike to the College, the University of London, and the world of learning, had edited, or published from his own pen, two volumes dealing with subjects of natural science. Professor Hearnshaw, as the reader will see from the notice which confronts the title-page, has already edited two volumes on matters of mediæval history. One of these volumes dealt with the social and political ideas of some great mediæval thinkers. The present book, which is in the nature of a continuation—though it is, of course, a separate and independent volume—is concerned with the ideas of some of the thinkers who inspired the age of the Renaissance and the Reformation.

I cannot but express the hope that the continuation will itself be followed by a continuation, and that we may receive from Professor Hearnshaw a further volume dealing with the social and political ideas of thinkers of a more modern age.

With the exception of the lecture on Luther by Professor J. W. Allen (who in this, as in the two previous volumes of lectures edited by Professor Hearnshaw, has been a generous contributor), the lectures printed in this volume are all the work of members of the staff of King's College. It would ill become me to blow up a trumpet in their praise ; nor

5

have they any need of a herald to announce their styles and titles. But I would say that they seem to me to have been fortunate in the themes they have found to their hand. They are concerned with the thinkers of a new age, in which a philosophy so accepted that it had become conventional, and a matter of rote, was being shed (though, as we find more and more, mediæval philosophy had such large elements of permanent truth that it cannot long be shed, but *usque recurret*), and in which, again, a freshness and novelty of view, as of a spring-time of the mind, naturally clothed thought and its expression. Nicolas of Cusa, it is true, like Sir John Fortescue, retains many elements of mediæval thought ; but Nicolas was also a scholar of the Renaissance and, for a time, an upholder of the revolutionary conciliar movement in the Church, and Sir John Fortescue, if he spoke in terms of Aquinas, was also the interpreter, or the forerunner, of modern English constitutionalism. Machiavelli, with a keen eye fixed in penetrating regard on the *verità effettuale delle cose* ; Sir Thomas More, steeped in Platonism and the social problems of a new age ; Erasmus, the would-be founder of a new and yet old *philosophia Christi*—all these have a brightness and a novelty which ages do not dim. Luther and Calvin shook the world of thought; their conceptions of State and society have influenced all succeeding generations, as well as their own. Each reader of this volume will choose for himself among these figures for his special study. But none, I venture to think, will more repay study than Nicolas of Cusa, whether his theme be of " learned ignorance " or of " catholic concordance," or, again, than Sir Thomas More, who, if he could persecute heretics, yet loved toleration, and international peace, and the cause of social justice.

ERNEST BARKER

6

CONTENTS

THE SOCIAL AND POLITICAL IDEAS OF SOME GREAT THINKERS OF THE RENAISSANCE AND THE REFORMATION

I

INTRODUCTORY

THE RENAISSANCE AND THE REFORMATION

I

IT is the fashion nowadays to deny the Renaissance and to decry the Reformation. ' Renaissance,' or re-birth, it is said, implies previous death, and throughout the Middle Ages there had been no death, but, on the contrary, a continuity of vigorous and prolific life. Similarly, ' Reformation,' or construction anew, connotes a return to a pristine purity of organisation and belief ; and, it is argued, the sixteenth century saw no such return, but rather the mere destruction of ancient institutions, the disintegration of venerable creeds, the stoppage of the process of divine evolution, and a return to (if anything) primordial chaos. These critical and unfavourable views of Renaissance and Reformation mark the extreme of the present-day reaction against the excessive protestantism of the seventeenth century and the exaggerated rationalism of the eighteenth.

The seventeenth century was an age of intense theological passion, of fierce religious persecution, of vivid memories of massacres and assassinations on behalf of the faith, of devastating civil wars between the adherents of conflicting creeds. In countries such as England, North Germany, and the Dutch Netherlands—where Protestantism prevailed—the Reformation was regarded as the breaking of a glorious dawn after a millennial night of unrelieved darkness, ignorance, and superstition. Even in countries—such as France, Spain, and Italy—where, after a sharp struggle, Catholicism re-established itself, the theologians and administrators of the new and dominant Order of Jesus regarded with some contempt the groping and puerile expositions of the cause of the Church which scholastic dialecticians had presented to the mediæval mind.

The eighteenth century—the self-styled Age of Reason—went farther than the seventeenth, and poured a sceptical disdain upon Catholic and Protestant alike. Representative thinkers of high eminence, such as Hume, Voltaire, and Goethe, rejected the whole Christian scheme of things, and professed faith in the unaided human intellect to solve the mystery of existence, and to furnish the spirit of man with a satisfying ethic and politic. It was at this time that the threefold division of history into ancient, mediæval, and modern was adopted, and at this time that the mediæval millennium received its disparaging designation, the Dark Ages. They were considered to be unworthy of study: they were a mere interlude of blackness between the dim light of classical antiquity and the high noon of eighteenth-century rationalism. " I know nothing of those ages which knew nothing," was the boast of one of the pundits of the period. Even Gibbon, who made it his business to know something of them, treated them with undisguised loathing and contempt. He lamented the fall of pagan Rome; he deplored the triumph of Christianity ; he regretted the incursion of the Teutons; he welcomed the Renaissance as a return to the sanity of the Hellenic world, and the

Reformation as, at any rate, a successful revolt against the obscurantism of the papal autocracy.

The hopes of the eighteenth-century rationalists were, however, doomed to disappointment. The empirical philosophers, the natural theologians, the utilitarian moralists, the political economists, the materialistic philanthropists, failed to satisfy the deeper spiritual needs of the time. The " enlightened despots " of the period, to whom social reformers looked for the salvation of mankind, proved to be but impotent fools, whose obvious imbecility was scarcely palliated by a doubtful benevolence. The eighteenth-century exaltation of intellect, at the expense of emotion and will, culminated in the French Revolution and the awful orgies with which Hébert and his fellow fanatics celebrated the worship of the Goddess of Reason on the desecrated altars of the church of Notre-Dame. Amid the horrors and abominations of Jacobin tyranny, and during the oppression of Rationalist persecution, the Romantic reaction was born. Religion resumed her sway over the minds of men. The emotion of worship and the will to believe reasserted themselves triumphantly against the discredited claims and presumptuous appeals of ineffective intellect. The tragedies of the quarter-century 1789–1815 were traced back to the disintegration of Christendom caused by the Reformation, and to the repudiation of spiritual authority associated with the Renaissance.

Protestantism—which had generally declined to unitarianism, deism, and agnosticism—was widely repudiated. Catholicism, both Roman and Anglican, was recalled to life in a marvellous outburst of energy. The Middle Ages once more were exalted, their study renewed, their writings re-edited and disseminated afresh, their glories depicted in glowing colours, their ideals reaffirmed, their institutions and practices re-established. Thus—to return to the point from which we started—the Renaissance was denied and the Reformation disparaged.

II

In this controversy between eighteenth-century Rationalists and nineteenth-century Romanticists where does the truth lie ? It would appear to lie midway between the two extremes.

On the one hand, the Middle Ages were by no means wholly dark or dead. It is true that they saw a decline in science, a decadence in art, a dearth in literature, accompanied by an invasion of barbarism, a recrudescence of superstition, a cessation of peace, a disappearance of comfort, a chronic prevalence of plague, pestilence, and famine, a deplorable falling away from the culture and humanity of the pagan world at its best. But, to set over against this, it is equally true that they saw, particularly in their central period (A.D. 604–1303), a vast elevation and purification of religion, an incalculably great exaltation and extension of morality, an immense advance in politics. They saw a pure and spiritual faith exorcise the demons which, under the names of divinities, the pagan masses had adored ; they saw the gentler virtues of brotherly kindness and love prevail over the sterner and more limited virilities called forth by sanguinary games and merciless war ; they saw the diminution of slavery, the mitigation of serfdom, the spread of freedom, the re-emergence of the individual, the growth of representative institutions, the development of government by debate, the gradual formation of national states dominated increasingly by an ever more articulate public opinion. Such was the by no means contemptible

12

heritage which the Middle Ages handed down to the modern world.

But, on the other hand, a renaissance was necessary, and a renaissance there was. It is true that at no time during the thousand years which intervened between the fall of Rome and the discovery of the New World had the spirit of man been wholly dead. At the very worst periods of barbarity and tumult the life of learning had been maintained, however feebly, in remote monasteries and sequestered cloisters. From time to time, moreover, during lulls in the æonian strife, revivals of scholarship had occurred. Not to mention the strange burgeonings of local culture, such as that of Ireland in the sixth century and of Northumbria in the eighth, there had been a widespread return to classical models and a notable expansion of education under the *Pax Romana* which Charlemagne succeeded in establishing and maintaining. This premature Renaissance was, unfortunately, but short-lived. It was nipped in its early promise by the renewed incursions of barbarians more ferocious and less assimilable than even those who had overthrown Old Rome—Vikings, Slavs, Magyars, Saracens. Not till the twelfth century did Christendom settle down again to moderate tranquillity. Then there transpired that remarkable movement known as the Latin Renaissance—a movement which showed how great and even magnificent was the vitality which lay at the heart of the mediæval civilisation. It was marked by, first, the revived and systematic study of the Roman Law; secondly, the formulation of the scholastic philosophy and theology; thirdly, the founding and development of the great universities; finally, the building and decoration of those most perfect embodiments of the mediæval genius, the Gothic cathedrals. The Latin Renaissance was not frustrated and rendered unfruitful, as had been the Carolingian

13

Renaissance, by any invasion of enemies from without. It was sterilised and destroyed from within by civil conflict and religious revolt. The mediæval mind, in fact, during the thirteenth century, was breaking away from the tutelage of the Church, and was seeking the open fields of specula- tion and adventure. But the power of the Church was great, and her ministers felt it to be their duty to maintain their challenged authority. Hence this century, together with the fourteenth, was a period of wild heresies and wanton schisms repressed by means of merciless in- quisitions and sanguinary crusades. The Middle Ages terminated in a welter of recrimination and bloodshed.

The Church suffered hardly less severely than the harassed and persecuted sects from the inquisitorial conflicts and anti-Christian crusades of the later Middle Ages. The decline of her beneficent influence may, indeed, be dated from the day when that most imperial and magisterial of Popes, Innocent III, launched the hosts of the destroyers against the devoted Albigenses (1208). The period which that lamentable event inaugurated was marked by unpre- cedented eccentricity and intractability of error, and by an answering rigidity and ferocity of orthodoxy. The Church, which in the early Middle Ages had led the way toward a rational interpretation of the mysteries of existence, and which in the central mediæval period had kept well abreast of the best science and philosophy of the time, now fell behind and became obscurantist and reactionary. Ideas began to reach Western Christendom from the Byzantine East, from Mohammedan Spain, from the Egyptian and Syrian Orient—ideas which could not be incorporated in the accepted body of divine theology, or harmonised with the standard creeds of Catholicism. St Thomas Aquinas and his school had continued to assert the unity of know- ledge, and to contend that all newly discovered truth of every

14

sort could be reconciled with revelation. Duns Scotus and his followers had felt constrained to divide truth into two compartments, putting on one side that which man by means of his reason is capable of perceiving and comprehending, but putting on the other side that which is sealed save to the eye of faith. This unsatisfactory dualism, although it enabled some amazing intellectual gymnastics to be accomplished in the fourteenth and fifteenth centuries, was manifestly impermanent: it was a mere temporary expedient to enable sceptics to escape combustion. As the number of the sceptics grew, and as the power of the Church to kindle bonfires diminished, the necessary unity of truth was reproclaimed, and the consequent falsity of the mediæval system of thought openly affirmed. This affirmation was the work of the Renaissance thinkers.

But not only was the Church of the later Middle Ages reactionary and obscurantist. It was also secular and corrupt. The fatal policy of Innocent III had committed it to the threefold worldly task of (1) superseding the Empire and establishing itself as the sole head of Christendom, (2) securing the feudal overlordship of the great European kingdoms, and (3) building up a powerful temporal state in Italy. This policy involved the Papacy, first, in a life or death conflict with the Imperial house of the Hohenstaufen; secondly, in ceaseless brawls with the growing power of the rising national kings, such as Edward I of England and Philip IV of France; thirdly, in ruinous and continuous war with Roman nobles, Neapolitan princes, and Lombard cities. In the course of these purely secular struggles the Papacy, and with it the Church, lost its spiritual and cosmopolitan character. It prostituted its supernatural powers—such as excommunication and interdict—to the base and transitory ends of war and diplomacy; it squandered the revenues provided by the faithful on military excursions and political intrigue; finally it sank to the level of a mere Italian principality, as cruel and perfidious as the worst. The depth of its degradation and impotence was seen when, during its Captivity at Avignon (1309–76), it became little more than an appendage to the French monarchy; and then, during the Great Schism (1377–1417), it became involved in suicidal civil war. There was evident need of a reformation, of an emancipation of the Church from the toils of the world, of a return to purity and spirituality, of a reaffirmation of the claims of personal religion and the necessity of righteousness of life.

III

The Renaissance of the fifteenth century may be considered in many aspects and regarded from various points of view. It was in a sense a " rebirth of the human spirit "; not, however, as we have remarked, in the sense of a return to life, but of an attainment of liberty. There had been no death of the spirit in the Middle Ages, but merely a thraldom to authority, a thraldom which was not only justifiable, but quite inevitable during the immaturity and juvenescence of the Teutonic peoples. The Church had, indeed, emancipated the barbarian invaders of the Roman Empire from the chains of a heavier thraldom; that is to say, from the bonds of innumerable and horrible superstitions—a veritable tyranny of devils—by which they were enslaved in their pre-Christian days. The creed which the Church imposed was incomparably more rational and more noble than the paganism which it expelled; and the yoke of the Christian priesthood in its best days was immeasurably lighter and kindlier than the burden imposed by the merciless devotees of the Nordic deities. Nevertheless, in the fifteenth century the Church had completed its pioneer educative work, and its rule had in its turn become an obstacle to the further development of the Western intellect. Thus the Renaissance may be regarded as the movement which marked the termination of the tutelage of the Teuton and his embarkation upon an independent, adventurous, and perilous career of unguided and unfettered speculation.

Again, the Renaissance may be viewed as the revolt of the lay mind against clerical control. The Church during the Middle Ages had safeguarded and transmitted some portion of the heritage of Greece and Rome. But it was a portion selected for theological reasons, and a portion from which the classical spirit was carefully and deliberately exorcised. The purification of Latin style by Petrarch (1304–74) was followed by a reperception of the classical spirit; by a search for and a discovery of countless long-lost masterpieces of Latin literature; by a recognition of the fact that Latin culture was based upon that of Greece; by a renewed study of the Greek language; by a zealous collection of Greek manuscripts from the libraries of the perishing Byzantine Empire; and by an ultimate reattainment of the Greek view of life. The Greek view of life was secular and pagan. In contradistinction to the mediæval view of life—which had envisaged man as fallen, human nature as depraved, the world as evil, the devil as dominant on earth, and the brief span of mortal existence as merely probationary to an eternity of bliss or woe—the Greek view had emphasised the goodness of man, the beauty and glory of the earth, the joy of existence, the insignificance of the supernatural, the all-importance of the present as compared with the irrecoverable past and the doubtful future.

The effect of this return to the pre-Christian attitude toward Man, Nature, and God, was an outburst of vernacular literature—poetry, drama, romance; a marvellous rejuvenation of art—painting, sculpture, architecture; and, above all, a revival of science, wherein the modern mind speedily outdistanced the most advanced discoveries and speculations of its ancient predecessors.

Italy was the first country in which this secularist and neo-pagan movement made its influence felt. In Italy the traditions of the Roman Empire had never wholly been broken; the Latin language had remained a living tongue; the Roman Law had retained its authority; the spell of the old religions had never been entirely cast off. Moreover, in the South, which so late as the eleventh century had continued under the political control of Constantinople, the Greek tongue had never ceased to be spoken, so that Calabria was the region to which Byzantine scholars naturally tended to migrate when the Turkish advance in the fourteenth and fifteenth centuries made their continuance in the East difficult or impossible. Barlaam, who tried to teach Greek to Petrarch, and Leontius Pilatus, who succeeded in teaching Greek to Boccaccio (1313–75), were both denizens of Constantinople who reached Florence by way of Calabria.

The Renaissance in Italy began as a humanistic revival. It was marked by (1) that purification of Latinity which we have noted as inaugurated by Petrarch. The papal secretaries of the fifteenth and sixteenth centuries—e.g., Valla, Manetti, Bembo, and Poggio—were particularly careful to reach and maintain a Ciceronian perfection of diction: a quality which, we may remark in passing, seemed to be regarded even by the Popes themselves as adequate compensation for anti-Christian beliefs and flagrantly immoral lives. The invention of printing and the multiplication of classical texts greatly extended the influence of the stylists, and gave rise both to criticism of the form and to widespread study of the substance of the writers of ancient

18

Rome. The purification of Latin was followed by (2) the recovery of Greek. The pioneer labours of Barlaam and Pilatus were continued much more systematically and effectively by Manuel Chrysoloras—who taught at Florence (1397–1400), and later at Pavia, Milan, Venice, and Rome —and by a host of successors, among whom Gemistos Plethon (*fl.* 1438) and John Lascaris (*d.* 1535) were perhaps the most notable. The printing of the Greek classics at the Aldine Press in Venice was an event of primary importance in the history of European culture. The dissemination of Latin and Greek literature, whether in manuscript or in type, was a challenge to study and discussion. Hence, as a further feature of the humanistic revival, we have to note (3) the founding of academies. Most notable of these was the Florentine Academy founded by Cosimo de Medici about 1458, and developed by his son Lorenzo the Magnificent. It was rendered illustrious by the activities of such members as Marsilio Ficino, Pico della Mirandola, Michelangelo, and Politian. The Roman Academy gave itself to the study of antiquities, and becoming thus political and revolutionary it had to be suppressed. The Neapolitan Academy, keeping clear both of philosophy which led to atheism and of politics which ended in republicanism, devoted its energies to purely literary pursuits. The Venetian Academy, closely associated with Aldo and his press, organised itself with admirable self-devotion and success to the preparation of critical editions of the Greek classics. The founding of academies was accompanied by (4) the formation of libraries. Specially noteworthy among these were the Medicean Library at Florence, the Vatican Library at Rome, the library of manuscripts collected by Federico da Montefeltro at Urbino, and the library primarily of Greek works, which Cardinal Bessarion—himself a convert from the Greek to the Latin communion—gave to the city of Venice in 1468. Finally, the humanistic revival necessitated (5) a remoulding of education. The mediæval *trivium* and *quadrivium*, intended to supply the foundation for the superstructure of theology, were found to be no longer adequate to bear the weight of the new learning, or to permit the manifestation of the classical spirit. The humanistic ideal of education was *not* to repress and subdue the natural faculties of a child, but to develop and enlarge them; *not* to inculcate asceticism, but to encourage athleticism; to achieve *not* self-abnegation, but self-realisation. Prominent among the pioneers of the new education were Vittorino da Feltre (1397–1446) and Guarino da Verona (1370–1460).

The humanistic revival was speedily followed by a renaissance in art. In sculpture and in architecture this renaissance took the form of a return to classical models. It was impossible to improve upon the perfection of the divine humanity revealed in the masterpieces of Phidias; it was difficult to build anything better or more beautiful than the gems which adorned the Acropolis or even the Capitol. In painting, however, there was a notable and original advance. Little of Greek or Roman painting was known. Painting had not been one of the dominant arts of antiquity; and such works as had been achieved had for the most part been wrought in fading colours and perishable materials, and so had been lost. Of mediæval painting there was enough, and more than enough. From the æsthetic point of view it was atrocious. It had not been intended to please the eye. Its purpose had been didactic; its form was deliberately conventional, like the letters of a modern alphabet; it had no closer a relation to nature than have the beasts and birds of heraldry. Mediæval painting lacked perspective; its pictures were devoid of depth; they had no background; they were relieved by no varieties of light

and shade ; their human figures were anatomical impossi-
bilities, no suggestion of vitality or mobility mitigating
their melancholy, statuesque, and everlasting hideousness ;
no feeling for nature lent a touch of charm to any fresco
or altar-piece. The dawn of the renaissance of painting
came with the Franciscan movement of the thirteenth
century. St Francis himself—by instinct a heretic, and
kept within the obedience of the Church only by his own
extraordinary peacefulness and humility, and by the unusual
wisdom and forbearance of Pope Innocent III—had heralded
the return to nature, by his tender love for birds and beasts,
and by his quick eye for beauty in mountain, wood, and
sea. The world to him was not the theologians' world,
incurably evil, hopelessly corrupt, dominated by the devil,
a mere snare to the senses of the would-be devout ; it was
a fair and pleasant world, eloquent of the glory of the
Creator, full of aids to worship, resonant with songs of praise.
The world, in short, as it presented itself to St Francis was
essentially the world as it had appeared to the artists of
antique Athens. The Franciscan feeling for nature was
soon caught by the painters. Cimabue began to depict
realistically the human form divine, as, for example, in
his Madonna in the church of Santa Maria at Florence
(1267). Giotto, a generation later, introduced backgrounds
of exquisite natural scenery in the twenty-eight frescoes
wherewith he adorned the church of St Francis at Assisi.
But it was the Franciscans, Fra Angelico and Fra Lippo
Lippi, who, at the end of the fourteenth and beginning of
the fifteenth century, marked the full return to nature and
humanity. With Botticelli (1447–1510) the classical influence became dominant : he painted Madonnas whose
proper name should have been Venus. This great painter
lived to see the life and work of the three still greater masters
of art whose achievements constitute the Golden Age of

the Italian Renaissance, viz., Leonardo da Vinci (1452–1515), Raphael (1483–1520), and Michelangelo (1475–1564).

Leonardo was wholly pagan in spirit, and Michelangelo, for all his preoccupation with prophets and saints, was primarily inspired by classical mythology. It is significant that one of Leonardo's pictures is said by some to represent John the Baptist, and by others Bacchus! It is equally significant that Michelangelo's great statue of Moses should be the perfect model of Olympian Jove. The same reversion to pre-Christian antiquity was evident in literature. Classical models were imitated in pastoral poems, satires, epics, dramas, epistles. Even in poems devoted to Christian themes the technical terminology of the Church was transmuted to most incongruous pagan equivalents: nuns became *vestales*; cardinals *augures*; St Peter and St Paul *dii tutelares Romæ*; the Christian Deity Himself *Jupiter Optimus Maximus*.

The study of Greek and Latin texts led in the natural course of things to the study of the original versions of the Old and New Testaments. The later Middle Ages had seen some attempts to get behind the readings of the Vulgate. Bishop Grosseteste of Lincoln, Friar Roger Bacon, the Dominicans of Paris, the Franciscans generally in the fourteenth century, John Wycliffe with the Lollards and Hussites who followed him—all had got themselves into trouble by prying behind the veil of the official Latin Bible. The period of the Renaissance, however, saw a movement which the Church was powerless to suppress. New texts of both Old and New Testaments were discovered; new translations were attempted; a new canon of criticism was applied by such eminent scholars as Lorenzo Valla. The serious study of Hebrew, with a view to the interpretation of the Talmud and the Old Testament, was undertaken by

such men as Pico della Mirandola and Reuchlin. Special-
ised research into the meaning of New Testament Greek
was made by a long line of learned students, among whom
Marsilio Ficino and Erasmus stand prominent. The history of the Church was reviewed and revised with sceptical
industry by such critics as the Magdeburg Continuators.

It will be noted that this religious aspect of the Renaissance was most evident north of the Alps. It was in the
Teutonic countries—Germany, Holland, England—rather
than in the Latin countries that the Renaissance took the
form of the Reformation.

IV

The Teutonic countries had for some time been alienated
from the Papacy. The causes of quarrel were mainly
secular : they concerned such matters as political control,
financial exactions, legal jurisdictions, administrative interference. The mediæval Church had become, especially
under Innocent III and his successors, a super-state exercising an authority which reduced all kings and princes to
a condition of vassalage. Papal legates dictated policy ;
papal collectors extracted sums of money which sometimes
exceeded the royal revenue ; papal courts called up cases
from the national tribunals ; papal provisions superseded
the customary rights of patronage ; papal penalties reduced
all resisters to submission. Under such powerful and
impartial pontiffs as Innocent III Latin countries had, of
course, suffered equally with Teutonic countries ; and all
of them, on the other hand, as a compensation for loss of
freedom and extortion of money, had benefited from the
strong and righteous rule of an effective international
authority. But both impartiality and righteousness had
vanished under Gregory IX and Innocent IV, when the

23

Papacy became involved in its mortal conflict with the Hohenstaufen. The Germans—princes, priests, and people alike—had come to regard the Roman Curia as their deadly and inveterate enemy, whom no concessions could conciliate and no conventions bind. This view had been emphasised during the Babylonish Captivity of the fourteenth century, when the Papacy became French and the Empire German. The embittered struggle between Pope John XXII and the Emperor Lewis the Bavarian had not been a conflict of the mediæval type between representatives of the two world-powers; it had been a Franco-German war of the modern sort. In this struggle England, under Edward III, had become involved. The Hundred Years War with France, which had begun in 1337, had found the Papacy wholly on the French side and largely under French control. It had been natural, therefore, that Edward III should make an alliance with Lewis the Bavarian; should accept the office of Imperial Vicar for the Rhenish provinces; should take German soldiers into his pay; should repudiate the tribute promised to the Papacy by King John; should limit papal patronage by the Statute of Provisors, and the appellate jurisdiction of the papal courts by the Statute of Præmunire. John Wycliffe's antagonism to the Papacy had commenced when, as agent of Edward III, he had gone to meet the papal commissioners at Bruges in order to rebut the papal claim to feudal overlordship over England, and to refuse the payment of the annual tribute which King John had promised in 1213.

The Reformation began, then, as a political movement at latest as far back as the thirteenth century. It is not fanciful, indeed, to trace premonitions of it some two centuries earlier, as, for example, in the three rules of William the Conqueror, and in the fulminations of the Salians during the Investiture Controversy. It was the revolt of the young Teutonic nations against the cosmopolitan authority of the Latin Church. In proportion as national consciousness increased, so also grew the unwillingness of laity and clergy alike to submit to the control and contribute to the support of an alien and doubtfully friendly power. The force behind the revolt of both Wycliffe and Huss was not Protestantism but Nationality. Neither the Englishman nor the Bohemian was so much the " Morning Star of the Reformation " as the herald of the modern state. Both were political agitators rather than religious pioneers.

The Reformation, however, had its religious side, but that displayed itself later. It was, indeed, a special feature of the fifteenth century. Just as the Babylonish Captivity of the Papacy generated national antagonism to the Gallicised Curia, so did the Great Schism, which immediately followed the return of the Popes to Rome (1377–1417), give rise to religious opposition. The spectacle of two, and finally three, rival pontiffs, each claiming universal dominion, each anathematising his rivals, and each exhausting the resources of the Church in suicidal civil war, was one which shocked the conscience and shook the faith of Christendom. There sprang up a cry for the calling of a General Council which should restore unity to the Church, purge it of corruption, and cleanse it from heresy. The Franciscans began to denounce the worldliness and wealth of the clergy, and to proclaim the dogma of apostolic poverty. The Lollards and others, going definitely beyond the bounds of orthodoxy, denied the doctrine of transubstantiation, on which was based the supernatural power of priests and prelates, and preached the priesthood of all believers and the sole sufficiency of the Scriptures to be the guide of life. The way was made straight for the appearance and the pronouncements of Luther.

V

When in 1517 Luther affixed his ninety-five theses to the door of the church at Wittenberg, both he and the world at large were astonished at the sensation which was caused and the consequences which were evoked. The theses were intended to be no more than a challenge to an ordinary academic disputation concerning an abstract theological problem. The subject, however, with which they dealt, viz., the ethics and the efficacy of Indulgences, was one which directly touched both the consciences and the account-books of the German people, and the controversy between doctors of divinity thus started developed into a war which involved the princes, nations, and races of the whole European continent. The theory of Indulgences, when carefully formulated in ecclesiastical Latin by theologians skilled in technical terminology, was not one calculated to outrage the moral sense of a mediæval Christian; it faithfully distinguished between the guilt and the penalty of sin, and studiously avoided trespassing upon the exclusive sphere of the divine prerogative. But the distinctions of the professors were lost upon the pious proletariat, and the virtues and validities of Indulgences as they were proclaimed by clerical travellers to credulous purchasers were taken to include not only remission of guilt but even licence to commit sin in the future. They were a source of moral degradation and also of considerable financial extortion of a fraudulent nature. They were, indeed, primarily an extraordinary means of transferring large sums of German money to the papal treasury. Their object was not the spiritual consolation of the Teutons, but the relief of the temporal embarrassments of an extravagant and corrupt Italian Court. Luther himself had visited Rome a few years earlier (1512), and he had been horrified at that spectacle of secularity and depravity which had long destroyed in the minds of thoughtful Italians all respect for the highly placed clergy, and all belief in the creed which they prostituted to the ends of luxury and lust. It was to maintain this corrupt and worldly hierarchy that the morals of Germany were being undermined and its hard-earned wealth drained away.

In challenging the theory and practice of Indulgences Luther had at first had no thought of revolt against either Church or Papacy. His appeal was to the conscience of the Church and the authority of the Pope. Not till 1519 did he realise how hopelessly the Curia had become committed to the vicious system of extravagance and extortion, or how difficult it was for the Church to withdraw from secular sovereignty and temporal possession. His famous disputation with Eck at Leipzig opened his eyes; while Eck's imprudent zeal and untimely dialectic skill drove him into overt rebellion by compelling him to appeal from the decisions of Councils and the commands of Popes to the teachings of the Fathers and the clear precepts of the Scriptures. The bull of excommunication naturally followed (June 1520). It was publicly burned, amid scenes of national enthusiasm, on December 10. Meantime Luther, in his three great Reformation writings, had (1) appealed "to the Christian Nobility of the German Nation"; (2) denounced " the Babylonish Captivity of the Church"; and (3) expounded his conception of " the Freedom of a Christian Man." The German people was roused as never before. If the Emperor Charles V had been a German he would possibly have been strong enough and unscrupulous enough to seize a unique opportunity of putting himself at the head of his subjects and converting his ramshackle empire into a powerful Protestant national state. But

Charles was not a German; and he *was* King of Spain, a country so zealously Catholic that any concession to heresy would infallibly have meant insurrection and expulsion. Hence Charles's course was predetermined for him. His first Imperial Diet, held at Worms (1521), ratified the excommunication of Luther and added its own ban. Papacy and Empire, the two great cosmopolitan and authoritarian institutions of the Middle Ages, were united to crush " the Nobility of the German Nation " and to suppress " the Freedom of the Christian Man."

Neither excommunication nor ban could be put into effect. Luther was protected alike from potent Papacy and impotent Empire by the princes and the people of Germany. Round him and his protest gathered all the discontents of the age. The Reformation became an increasingly composite movement. Politically, as we have seen, it was a revolt of the Teuton against Latin domination, and also a rebellion of princes and cities against Imperial control; socially, it was a rising of the oppressed against their lords, ecclesiastical and civil; economically, it was a secularist assault upon the accumulated wealth of the Church; ecclesiastically, it was an insurrection of the laity against the clergy; morally, it was a protest against the degeneracy of the priesthood and the flagrant separation of religion from ethics; theologically, it was a return to the New Testament, to personal piety, and to the simplicity of the doctrine of justification by faith; intellectually, it was a revolt of the individual against authority, and a reassertion of the right of freedom of thought. The strongest element in the Reformation, however, remained that which had been the earliest, viz., the political. The Reformation— that is to say, the disruption of mediæval Christendom— was the first great achievement of the modern national state. It need not have been accompanied by a violent change in creed or by a conspicuous abandonment of venerable ritual. That it was so accompanied was largely due to the deplorable accidents that Eck was injudicious, Luther outrageous, and Pope Leo X a worldling incapable of comprehending the issues at stake. But in any case Christendom would have been disintegrated, and Anglican, Gallican, Germanic, Spanish, and other churches set up, on the Byzantine model, under the control of national kings. Even as it was, Philip II of Spain and Louis XIV of France, good Catholics as they were, exercised hardly less authority over their clergy than did Henry VIII of England. The fall of the Papacy from its mediæval eminence was as evident in Catholic countries as in Protestant.

Whether a country should remain Catholic or become Protestant would seem to have been determined mainly by political considerations. For instance, England became definitely Protestant under Elizabeth in order to shake off its dependence upon Spain ; Sweden became Protestant in order to recover its autonomy from Denmark ; Scotland adopted Calvinism in order to sever its embarrassing connexion with France ; the Dutch Netherlands rose in religious revolt because they were determined to repudiate the political authority of Philip II. In France the Huguenot cause was taken up by the feudal nobility and the autonomous Communes, in order that it might add strength to their arms in their struggle to maintain their mediæval privileges against the encroachments of the centralising Crown ; and it was this unhappy alliance of French Protestantism with what was a reactionary, unprogressive, anti-patriotic, and anti-national movement which led to its ultimate and complete extinction. Similarly, Protestantism in Spain identified itself with the unpopular causes of Moors and Jews, and with the anachronistic claims of ancient towns and provinces to impossible liberties ; hence

29

it was suppressed by fire and sword amid the plaudits of the populace.

It is noteworthy that before the end of the sixteenth century the permanent lines between Protestant states and Catholic states had been drawn. Since that time no state has transferred its allegiance from the one camp to the other.

VI

The immense changes effected in Western Europe by the Renaissance and the Reformation inevitably had consequences of profound importance in the sphere of social and political ideas. Mediæval Christendom had been, in theory if not in fact, a unitary commonwealth under the dual authority of Pope and Emperor, each representing one aspect of the Divine Majesty wherein ultimate sovereignty resided. Within that commonwealth the interests and activities of the individual were subordinated to the good of the Christian community as a whole. The fifteenth and sixteenth centuries witnessed the break-up of that ideal commonwealth and the abandonment of its sacred communism. The Renaissance saw the establishment of the secular state as the primary political unit; the Reformation saw the emergence of the individual as his own philosopher and priest. Hence, obviously, political and social theory had to be completely recast to fit the new situation. The lectures contained in this volume give some indication of the processes of the thought of the period. Nicolas of Cusa and Sir John Fortescue lived in the fifteenth century, when peaceful and evolutionary reform seemed not impossible. Both of them contemplated developments of constitutional government which would not involve any breach with the past. Machiavelli bridged the two eras and,

THE RENAISSANCE AND THE REFORMATION

wholly rejecting the mediæval system, devoted his great powers and wide knowledge to the task of formulating the policy of the new national state. Sir Thomas More, faithful to the Catholic ideal, was eager to lessen the social hardships which the age of transition entailed. Erasmus, for his part, was anxious to ease the intellectual pains which the advent of the new learning was everywhere causing. Luther and Calvin, leaders of the revolt against the Papacy, were compelled by the necessities of their position to formulate new political principles for the guidance of their followers.

THE EDITOR

BIBLIOGRAPHY

ACTON, LORD : *Lectures on Modern History.* 1906.
BEARD, C. : *The Reformation in Relation to Modern Thought.* 1883.
BURCKHARDT, J. : *The Renaissance in Italy.* (English translation, 1878.)
Cambridge Modern History, vols. i and ii. 1902–3.
HUDSON, W. H. : *The Story of the Renaissance.* 1912.
HULME, E. M. : *Renaissance and Reformation.* 1915.
OLDHAM, J. B. : *The Renaissance.* 1912.
PATER, W. : *The Renaissance.* 1873.
SEEBOHM, F. : *The Era of the Protestant Revolution.* 1874.
SICHEL, EDITH : *The Renaissance.* 1914.
STONE, J. M. : *Reformation and Renaissance, A.D. 1377–1610.* 1904.
SYMON, J. D., and BENSUSAN, S. L. : *The Renaissance and its Makers.* 1913.
SYMONDS, J. A. : *The Renaissance in Italy.* 1875–86.
TANNER, E. M. : *The Renaissance and the Reformation.* 1908.
TAYLOR, H. O. : *Thought and Expression in the Sixteenth Century.* 1922.

NICOLAS OF CUSA

FEW that enter the cool cloister of Santa Maria Novella in Florence are unmoved by the Dominican ideal of the Church militant and triumphant painted on the walls of the Spanish Chapel. On the eastern side are seen sitting on twin thrones in front of Santa Maria del Fiore the universal bishop and the universal emperor. On either hand are arrayed the great dignitaries of Church and Empire in a descending order; and at the feet of the two powers of Christendom are gathered the sheep and lambs of Christ's flock guarded by the black and white hounds of the Lord. On the opposite wall is St Thomas Aquinas surrounded by angels, prophets, and saints; in his hand the open book of his doctrine, under his feet the heretics Arius, Sabellius, and Averroes in attitudes of rueful discomfiture. For his was the theory that perfected and rounded the Church's all-embracing system of politics and culture, that *Wunderkreise* or miraculous circle of institutional life based on tradition, the sacraments, and worldwide spiritual jurisdiction, in which the believer was born, nourished, and conducted to the bliss that Andrea Orcagna had depicted on the walls of the Strozzi Chapel within. A little more than twenty years after the painting of this mediæval system the fiercest reaction against it was raging. The Great Schism, attacking the very centre of unity, had broken out; heretical movements were aflame in Southern Germany and the Rhineland, while Waldensian congregations were multiplying in the eastern provinces of the

32

Empire;[1] above all, there were growing up independently
minded communities of radical individualists that took
the Gospel and undirected reason as their guides, the
' sect-type '—Wycliffe, Huss—which, in the distinction
so finely drawn by a great scholar and critic, stands
in fundamental opposition to the ' Church-type ' in the
history of the Christian ideal working itself out in social
form.[2] The republican organisations of the towns, the
growth of national sentiment in England and (to a lesser
degree) in France, the Land Leagues in Germany and the
Spaniard in Naples, were proving too strong for the political
claims of the Church, weak from the long years at Avignon.
Her guardianship of the economic and the intellectual
life of the people was passing into the hands of laymen :
her moral influence was impaired by the fiscal rapacity of
the Curia and the crying need for internal reform. By
the end of the fourteenth century the great pictures in the
Spanish Chapel bear the character of dream.

To make the harmony portrayed in them a reality once
again and so re-establish the moral and spiritual forces of
the Church was the aim of the Conciliar Movement. Its
history is that of a great and unsuccessful attempt to apply
to one of the enthroned powers the enlightened constitutional remedies of the time, on the assumption that the
Church, as a polity, was, in Gierke's words, "charged with
the mission of realising the ideal of a perfect political constitution."[3] To terminate the schism, to absorb the sect
in the unity of the whole, to reform the Church in head and
members by the method of universal representative councils
—these were the means to the end ; the remedial principle,

[1] L. Pastor, *History of the Popes*, i, 157–158.
[2] E. Tröltsch, *Die Soziallehren der christlichen Kirchen und Gruppen*, pp. 368–
374. The 'Church-type' (*Kirchentypus*) is all-claiming, objective, institutional ; the 'sect-type' (*Sektentypus*) is restricted to groups, subjective, mystic,
dependent on direct personal relations with God and between its members.
[3] *Political Theories of the Middle Age* (tr. Maitland), p. 49.

the (to us) familiar one that no government is absolute, but is founded on the voluntary consent of the governed. This —which is in the last resort the idea of popular sovereignty— may have been derived partly from the peculiarly Germanic idea of the Fellowship (*Genossenschaftsidee*), which, to quote Gierke once more, is based on the " aboriginal and active Right of the group taken as a Whole " ;[1] partly from an interpretation of the *Lex Regia* by the Glossators, who found in the *Corpus Juris* the express indication that the will of the people was the source of rulership ;[2] and partly from the contractual element in feudalism with its inherent notions of compact and consent as the condition of the tenure of office or power.[3] Howsoever the idea was compounded, it is sufficient at present to note that many of the arguments which in earlier days were used by Churchmen against Imperial claims are now in a slightly varied form applied by their successors to the basis of ecclesiastical power. The novelty and interest of the experiment lies in the application of constitutional ideas to an institution which by its outward nature seemed, and in its inmost heart knew itself to be, antagonistic both to the principle and to the organisation they involved. Yet that way seemed to lie the only hope of reform. The solution of the difficulty called for the finest intelligence, the most far-sighted sympathy with the opposing positions. We shall see in what measure they were given.

The subject of this essay made his contribution to that solution. But he did more : once the issue had been decided

---

[1] *Political Theories of the Middle Age* (tr. Maitland), p. 37.

[2] In the famous text (*Dig.*, i, 4, and *Inst.*, i, 2, 6) : " Quod principi placuit legis habet vigorem : utpote cum lege regia, quæ de imperio eius lata est, *populus ei et in eum omne suum imperium et potestatem conferat*" (Gierke, *op. cit.*, pp. 142 *n.*, 147.

[3] On the question of the doctrine of popular sovereignty in the Conciliar Movement some helpful remarks are to be found in F. von Bezold, " Lehre von der Volksuveränität," *Historische Zeitschrift*, vol. xxxvi, especially pp. 351–358.

against his early line of argument, by a change of front often too lightly condemned he became a protagonist of the papal party. In doing so he was forced to depart for a time from the great aim of his life, that of harmonising conflicting tendencies in the Church. His career is of a man with a passion for unity and peace, which found its root in a philosophy of reconciliation almost Hegelian in its comprehensiveness; yet of a man not infrequently led by the stress of bitter and determined opposition into action inconsistent with that unifying thought. Herein lies a difficulty for our immediate purpose. A summary account, however careful, of one or two of his chief political works will only very partially convey an impression of what he meant to his contemporaries; the whole course of his life forms a study so helpful toward an understanding of the strength and weakness of the Conciliar party and the character of the papalist reaction that to stop short at his best-known work, the *Catholic Concord*—an essay of early manhood before the lines of his activity were fixed and while his thought was still fluid—would be inadequate. Moreover, in order to see him as he was it is essential to mark the dominant principle of his philosophy, a task which cannot be attempted if we concentrate solely on his political views. It is for these reasons that I have tried, too perfunctorily, I fear, the way of biography rather than of ' political science '; and in so doing must frankly acknowledge my debt to M. Edmond Vansteenberghe, whose work on Cusanus, with its thorough examination of the sources for his life and writings, no student of the early period of humanism can afford to neglect.

Nicolaus Cancer de Cusza, as a Heidelberg document calls him, was born in 1401 at Cues, opposite Berncastel, in a bend of the Moselle. Not far from the graceful Gothic hospice of St Nicholas, his foundation and gift to that home of vineyard and meadow, can be seen the house where his father, John Khrypffs (or Krebs), a boatman, lived in moderate comfort. Nicolas, destined for his father's trade, was to follow other paths. A passion for study led him at the age of twelve to leave his home for the house of the friendly Count Theodorich of Manderscheid, who in all probability sent him for his education to the Brothers of the Common Life at Deventer.[1] This was the institute kept by the successors of Gerard de Groot and Florence Radewyn, a school famous for its intellectual and moral standards, where the study of history and of the classics was not forgotten, and pupils were encouraged to read deeply and take careful note of what they read. The training there must have left its mark upon the future cardinal. At the age of sixteen he passed to the University of Heidelberg, matriculating the year after the Council of Constance had voted its decrees proclaiming the superiority of the General Council over the Pope, the condemnation of John Huss, and the institution of the first commission of ecclesiastical reform. Like most of their teachers the students of Heidelberg were enthusiastically on the side of Conciliar reform, and to some the Parliamentary *régime* foreshadowed at Constance seemed to hold out prospects of a career. But a young man ambitious to make a mark in Conciliar politics would first have to learn some law and, above all, the arts of the speaker. Such considerations— but doubtless also pure intellectual curiosity and the desire to breathe an air which has ever captivated his young compatriots—may have led Nicolas in October 1417 to enrol himself as a student in the faculty of law at the University

[1] This has been contested by J. Marx, *Nicolaus von Cues und seine Stiftungen zu Cues und Deventer*, p. 140. The view here is that of Vansteenberghe, *Le Cardinal Nicolas de Cues*, pp. 6 (note 3) and 7. On the *Fraterherren* see the article of K. Hirsche in Herzog's *Realencyklopädie*, 2nd ed., ii. 678–760, which gives a bibliography.

36

of Padua, a school famous for its canonists and also at the time for its scientists, mathematicians, and humanists. Vittorino da Feltre was there, probably Filelfo, and there too Giuliano Cesarini, whose noble features and distinguished mind would first reveal to the young Teuton the meaning of the Latin genius. Padua was near Venice, the gateway to the East, which had among its professors a first-rate Hellenist, Ugo Benzi of Siena. At Padua Nicolas could listen to a well-known teacher of music and astrology (*i.e.*, mathematics and astronomy), Prosdocimo de' Beldomandi, and to the scientist Paolo del Pozzo Toscanelli, to whom he was later to dedicate his *De Transmutationibus Geometricis*. In this atmosphere he laid the foundation of that remarkable mathematical and scientific knowledge for which he became as justly celebrated as for his theology.[1] In 1423 he took his doctorate in canon law, and in 1424 paid his first visit to Rome, which Martin V, the Pope whose election in 1417 ended the Great Schism, had been busy for six years in cleansing and restoring, where also St Bernardino of Siena could be seen recalling the inhabitants to the virtues of the past. On returning to his native diocese Nicolas was given for his support a canonry at St Simeon at Trier and the cure of Altrich (though he was not yet in priest's orders), and soon began to be recognised as an authority on canon law; so much so that soon, in 1426, he was discovered by, and attached as a secretary to, Giordano Orsini, the papal legate in Germany. Orsini was a good example of the opulent *cardinal lettré*, a patron

[1] One may instance his projects for the reform of the calendar in 1436–7 ; his corrections in the astronomical tables of Alphonso X of Castille ; his map of Central Europe (*cf.* A. E. Nordenskjöld, *Facsimile Atlas to the Early History of Cartography*, tr. J. A. Ekelöf) ; his hygrometer (*De Staticis Experimentis*, p. 176) and experiments in weighing ; his studies in dynamics (*cf.* P. Duhem, *Léonard de Vinci*, t. ii) ; and, above all, the geometrical writings, the *De Transmutationibus Geometricis* (1450) cited above, the *Quadratura Circuli* (1450), the *De Mathematicis Complementis* (1453), and the *De Mathematica Perfectione* (1458).

of letters who contended with the young humanists in his
retinue, often far cleverer than himself, in the pursuit and
discovery of manuscripts of the classics. The post brought
Nicolas the deanery of Coblenz and friendship with a
number of Italian humanists; for the young scholar and
researcher had aroused their curiosity by his discoveries,
both real and imagined, in German libraries, the best being
that of a manuscript of Plautus containing sixteen comedies.[1]
Some of his eager correspondents he was to meet later at
the Great Council which was to mark the turning-point of
his career.

For the turning to classical antiquity was but one aspect
of the movement toward new valuations in the life of the
spirit, which in the spheres of criticism and æsthetic we
call the Renaissance, and in that of religious thought, when
it ultimately came, the Reformation. From the end of
the fourteenth century the magic word reform had been on
all lips. The abject state of the Church during the Schism
and the disorganisation of the Empire had either brought
men to a sort of millenarianism, expectation of the end of
the world and the coming of Antichrist, or had caused them
to look forward to the betterment of society, to a reign
of order, justice, and tranquillity. To the latter type, the
optimists, not only the reform of the Church in head and
members, which was urgently and universally demanded,
but also the whole cause of international peace seemed to
be at stake in the trial of the great experiment of reform
by a representative council. The Council at Constance
did at least restore unity; but peace had not been forth-
coming. The question of sovereignty in the Church had
been raised; and where some sort of federalism was the
only hope, an absolutist Pontiff and an ultramontane party
reacting strongly against the decree *Frequens* had made its

[1] Now Cod. Vat. Latin. 3870.

appearance. Opposed to it, suspicious and intractable, stood a party of democratic leanings, which under the leadership of Cardinal Louis Aleman was to fight for the continued existence of the Council as the supreme organ of government and jurisdiction in the Church. It was these opposing forces which the presidential tact of Cesarini and the pen of Nicolas of Cues sought to reconcile at Basel. The task was formidable; for after the first session Eugenius IV, who in 1432 succeeded Martin V, issued a bull of dissolution which aroused the strongest antipathies among the extreme Conciliar elements, while the problem of the recalcitrant Bohemians was still unsolved and remained like a thorn in the flesh of the moderates. It was certain that the ultramontanes would call in question the competence of a council continued against the express prohibition of the Pope: it was equally certain that the radicals or democrats, heading for a nationalism in religion which spelled anarchy, would forget the historical development of the Papacy, lose the sense of unity which the primacy of Rome ensured, and try to break with the past. Thirty, however, is the age of courage and vast horizons, and, confident in his powers, Nicolas, summoned to it on other business, put forward to the Council of Basel at the end of 1433 a reasoned statement of conclusions upon the power of ecclesiastical Councils combined with a programme of reform both in Church and Empire. Called *De Concord-antia Catholica*, the conclusions and the programme of action aim at achieving harmony between the warring interests. The point of view, however, is none the less definite, and places its author at the end of the line of publicists such as Henry of Langenstein, Conrad of Gelnhausen, Gerson, and Pierre d'Ailly, who prepared the way for the Council. The methods of these men were admirably characterised by Dr Figgis:

They rest on a historical development of realised fact. They appear to have discerned more clearly than their predecessors the meaning of the constitutional experiments which the last two centuries had seen in considerable profusion, to have thought out the principles that underlay them, and based them upon reasoning that applied to all political societies; to have discerned that arguments applicable to government in general could not be inapplicable to the Church. In a word they raised the constitutionalism of the past three centuries to a higher power; expressed it in a more universal form and justified it on grounds of reason, policy, and Scripture. This is why it seems truer to regard the movement as mediæval rather than modern in spirit.[1]

But there is perhaps a trifle more opportunism in the *Catholic Concord*; Nicolas is a profound student of the Fathers and of the acts of the early Councils, and he has his history at his fingers' ends;[2] he is ready to substantiate his views therewith, but his eyes are fastened on the assembled Fathers in the Council and on the antagonisms which he has to allay. He must conciliate the two tendencies: he must, as M. Vansteenberghe puts it, " bind the present movement to the historical past of the Church ";[3] but he must also go forward as a man of his age who has been influenced by the spirit of democratic independence running strong in the Rhineland. Characteristically, therefore, in a work whose keynote is harmony and peace he seeks to unite past and present—historically, by pointing to the continuous inspiration of the Holy Spirit in the Church throughout the ages; ideally, by demonstrating in mystical symmetry the complete interconnexion of each part of the

---

[1] *From Gerson to Grotius*, p. 47.
[2] *Cf.* his criticism of Marsilius of Padua for saying that there is no need to accept the doctors of the Church as authority except in so far as they base themselves on Biblical canon : " Hæc est perniciosa opinio post sanctæ Ecclesiæ approbationem probabilium doctorum " (*De Concordantia Catholica*, II, xxxiv, in *Nicolai de Cusa Opera*, Basel, 1565, p. 775. Future references here are to the Basel edition).
[3] *Le Cardinal Nicolas de Cues*, p. 35.

great Christian system, militant, expectant, triumphant—
and at the same time to advance the Conciliar interest
through a critique of the nature and origin of ecclesiastical
power.

The Church, he writes, is a living unity. It is a fra-
ternity,[1] united to the one Lord, from whom, " the peaceful
king of infinite concord, that sweet agreement or spiritual
harmony flows in due order and proportion into all its
subject and united members, that God may be all in all." [2]
Tripartite in form, it is triumphant, asleep (*dormientem*, or
in Purgatory) and militant; [3] organic in constitution, it
has spirit, soul, and body, the counterpart of which in
heaven is the Trinity, the angels, and the blessed, on earth
the sacraments, the priesthood, and the faithful. As in
the heavenly, so in each one of these earthly divisions there
is hierarchy and perfect gradation ; in the sacraments from
the lowest to the supreme service of the Eucharist, in the
priesthood from the subdeacons up to the Supreme Pontiff,[4]
among the faithful from counts and governors through the
margraves, dukes, and kings up to the Emperor himself.[5]
The harmonious symmetry, everywhere threefold, is complete.

To the *sacerdotium*, the soul of the Church, Books I and II
are devoted. Just as in each diocese unity is secured by
the bishop, so in the whole Church it is ensured by the
Pope. He is *episcoporum princeps*, the captain in the army

[1] *De Conc. Cath.*, I, v, 698 : " Quoniam Ecclesia ab unitate et concordantiali
congregatione dicitur, . . . ipsa ex fraternitate constituitur."
[2] I, i, 692.
[3] I, v, 699. The connexion he gives thus : " Dormiens Ecclesia, tanquam
media inter angelos et homines, considerata est ut umbra angelicæ [*i.e.*,
triumphantis], et militans ut umbra dormientis : licet dormiens ab humana
viatrici Ecclesia non separatur quousque traducatur in triumphantem."
[4] I, vi, 700–viii, 703.
[5] III, i, 780 : " Cuius [the *corpus*] gradualis hierarchica ordinatio in unum
principem, ab infimo simplicium laicorum, pedum typum gerentium, per
Rectores, Comites, Marchiones, Duches et Reges usque in Cæsareum caput,
ex superioribus facile quisquam intelligere poterit."

of Christ.[1] His position, however, has gradually evolved. He holds his primacy in virtue of a definition of the Council of Chalcedon, which having regard to the antiquity of Rome gave its bishop the first place and the bishop of Constantinople the second.[2] Out of the five early patriarchal sees the Roman in the course of time came to the head owing to its age, its dignity, its line of martyrs, as well as to divine privilege.[3] But when we speak of the *Church* we may mean not only the Pope or the Pope and cardinals, but all the churches united under and subject to Rome or Constantinople as the case may be. The union of these churches is called by the Greeks a Synod, by us a Council. The nature and power of such Councils calls for our investigation.

Nicolas does it in two principal ways. He distinguishes carefully between the various types of Council; and he discusses the meaning of the *plenitudo potestatis* claimed by the successors of St Peter. No assembly, he argues, can be termed a General Council which does not comprise the Pope or his legate. The Pope has the right of summoning and presiding over the Council; but if having done so he refuses to associate himself with its work, the assembly may after due and proper interval (for it must never act precipitately) continue without him, although it cannot decide questions of faith without his participation; *materia fidei Papam exigit.*[4] But the expression ' General Council ' needs definition. There are two types, which have not always been properly distinguished. There is the General

---

[1] I, xv, 708 : " Quare ita ut Petrus princeps fuit Apostolorum, ita et Romanus Pontifex episcoporum princeps, quoniam in locum Apostolorum episcopi succedunt. . . . Unde iste principatus est super omnes homines in Ecclesia existentes, qui per fidem constituitur, est enim capitaneus in eo exercitu."   [2] I, xvi, 708.

[3] I, xvi, 710 : " Concludendum, existimo, Romanam sedem, ob sæculi dignitatem, et divinum prævilegium, et in augmentum fidei, ut pax servaretur, et ob tot experimenta sanctorum præsulum, quorum successive plusquam triginta propter fidem martyris coronabantur ; per Conciliorum statuta primatum merito possidere."   [4] I, ii, 712–713.

Council in which the Pope sits as patriarch, the *Concilium Universale Patriarchale*, which is always subordinate to the Pontiff and cannot sit in judgment upon him unless he goes wrong in matters of faith, when he may be corrected by the anathema and the withdrawal of obedience;[1] and there is the General Council of the representatives of the whole body of the·Church, the *perfectissima Synodus*, which is without doubt above the Pope. As Vicar of Christ the Pope presides over the whole Church, but his authority is of human, as well as of divine, origin, for historically the *primitivitas* or primacy, in virtue of which he wields his power, derives in part " from men and from the canons," as has been shown.[2] In the second place, the bishops do not derive their jurisdiction from the Pope. St Peter received from Christ no more power than the other Apostles; " nothing was said to Peter that was not said to the others also." From a jurisdictional point of view all bishops are equal, as they were in the days of the Apostles. The Pope's superiority lies simply in his administrative powers. St Peter was, and so his successor is, *maior in administratione*—a very important point.[3] The Pope's position, therefore, is like that of the Principal or Rector of a university, who cannot legislate apart from his Senate.[4] In

[1] I, vii, 718–720.

[2] I, xvii, 735–736 : " Hoc nobis sufficit quod licet Romanus Pontifex ut successor Petri a Christo magna habeat prævilegia et altam potestatem ex sede et Cathedra, quæ prævilegia cum sede stabilia sunt : tamen primitivitas illa, qua Romanus Pontifex primus est omnium Ecclesiarum, partim etiam ab hominibus et canonibus est, iuxta superius dicta."

[3] I, xiii, 727–729.

[4] I, xviii, 739–740 : " Verum quia universale Concilium est congregatio sive Ecclesia, de membris universæ catholicæ Ecclesiæ congregata, et repræsentat ex hoc universam Ecclesiam : tunc considerandum est, quod Romanus Pontifex etiam habet figuratam et repræsentivam personam, unius universæ Ecclesiæ." But the Synod's representation is far less " confused " than the Pontiff's, and therefore its judgment is more infallible: "Non dubium quanto illa Synodus minus confuse plus tenendo in veritate repræsentat, tanto eius iudicium plus a fallibilitate versus infallibilitatem tendit, et semper maius est iudicio unici Romani Pontificis, eum [? eam = Ecclesiam] confusissime figurantis."

the third place, the Synod represents more clearly and infallibly than the Pope the Universal Church which in itself possesses the power of binding and loosing and through Christ's presence is indeviable and infallible. The voice of the Council is the unanimous voice of the Church Universal, and this unanimity is a sure sign of the presence of the Holy Spirit within it.[1] It stands for the whole body of bishops, to whom equal powers of jurisdiction have descended. The Pope is not the universal bishop, but first among the others ; and the authority of the Council is to be founded not in the Pope, but in the consent of all.[2] For it is by consent that leadership or rulership exists.[3] Papal authority is derived from the consent and agreement of the whole body of the Church, and that body in the persons of its representatives may therefore, in case of necessity, and for offences other than heresy, take action and depose the Pope when he does not fulfil the administrative function expected of him—when he is, in fact, *inutilis*.[4] Conversely, the Pope cannot change or resist the canons of General Councils, to which he is demonstrably inferior. This particularly applies to the decrees of Constance and of the second session of Basel. At first, it is true, there were doubts about the legality of these assemblies

[1] II, iii, 713.

[2] II, xiii, 730 : " Papa non est universalis episcopus, sed super aliis primus, et sacrorum Conciliorum non in Papa, sed in consensu omnium vigorem fundamus."

[3] II, xiv, 730 : " Omnis constitutio radicatur in iure naturali : et si ei contradicit, constitutio valida esse nequit. . . . Unde cum natura omnes sint liberi, tunc omnis principatus, sive consistat in lege scripta, sive viva apud principem est a sola concordantia et consensu subiectivo." We might almost think ourselves in the days of Rousseau. *Cf.* I, xv, 731 : " Constat omnium constitutionum ligandi vigorem consistere in concordia et consensu tacito vel expresso."

[4] II, xvii, 736 : " Quis dubitare potest sanæ mentis, absque veræ potestatis et privilegii sedis diminutione, universale concilium tam in abusum quam abutentem potestem habere pro sui ipsius conservatione et totius Ecclesiæ salutari ordinato regimine ? . . . Quare universaliter dici potest universale Concilium, repræsentationem catholicæ Ecclesiæ, habere potestatem immediate a Christo et esse omni respectu tam supra Papam quam sedem apostolicam."

44

owing to the troubles and discords at their inception. But their eventual unanimity has been a clear sign of the in-dwelling of the Holy Spirit. Now the second session of Basel, in spite of the bull of dissolution, has held resolutely to its course and unanimously drawn the conclusion that the Pope is bound to accept the reforming decrees and cannot suppress or change them. "The Holy Spirit has dictated the syllogism": the Pope is therefore bound to obey the reforming decrees: he cannot quash them. *Papa constitutionibus generalis concilii contradicens non auditur*.[1]

The conclusion thus rests on a fourfold foundation: that the Papacy is an administrative function; that all power, spiritual as much as temporal, is dependent on the consent of the whole body over which it is exercised; that that consent is conveyed through representatives; and that the representatives of the whole body, in this instance the Church, are the Council.[2] But the position is guarded with calm reasonableness. The assembly at Basel must pro-ceed toward the Pontiff with the greatest moderation, and avoid all suspicion of arrogance. It must work peacefully for the interest of the faith and the good of the Catholic Church as a whole.[3] The concord must be constructive, and Nicolas accordingly proceeds to give his proposals for reform. The *difformitas* or disorder in the Church springs, he says, from our digression from the order handed down

---

[1] II, xx, 748.

[2] For the sake of brevity I have omitted the discussion of the Pope's ἐπιείκεια or power of dispensation on grounds of equity; he can only use it, Nicolas says, if there is really just and adequate reason; it is because the Council of Basel found the reasons put forward in the bull of dissolution inadequate that it declared that instrument contrary to the decree *Frequens* (II, xx, 749).

[3] II, xx, 751 : " Quare hoc sacrum Concilium, absque passione cum summa mansuetudine se habere debet in ordine ad Romanum Pontificem, non se ex privilegio universalis Concilii in tantum erigat (de quo potius dolendum esset) quod obliviscatur subiectionis Patriarchalis in qua semper fuit, secun-dum quam in Papam fidelem nihil posset: sed servato debito honore cuncta pacifice in augmentum fidei, et divini cultus et universale bonum catholice Ecclesiæ unanimi concordantia ordinentur, ut videantur opera nostra bona et glorificetur Deus pater qui est in cælis."

to us by the Fathers, from the failure of each part to do its duty.[1] What is wanted is obedience to existing canons, not a mass of new legislation: *non deficiunt canones sed executiones.* He diagnoses accurately the sickness of the fifteenth-century Church—the absence of the sense of vocation, lack of governance, evasion of duty. The Fourth General Council of Constantinople decreed that metropolitans must not exercise their offices through others, but must attend personally to their work, and not become secularised. That decree might well be applied more generally.[2] The head of the Church and his subordinates must be united by a veritable spiritual marriage, and marriage implies consent on both sides; the faithful should therefore as far as possible elect their priests, the priests their bishops with the consent of their congregations, the bishops their metropolitan with the priests' help, and the metropolitans their cardinals.[3] To avoid the reproach of avarice in the Curia, all fees must be abolished: and instead there should be an annual collection to defray the cost of ecclesiastical administration.[4] Most interesting of all is the proposal for a permanent advisory Council elected from the Provinces which should assist the Pope and Council when local difficulties called for solution.[5] Commends and pensions should be abolished, the number of small benefices reduced by amalgamation, and pluralism reduced.[6]

After the soul, the body. The third book is devoted to the Empire. Civil society, of which the most preferable governmental type is elective monarchy, in order to be harmonious should be graded and articulated like the Church.

---

[1] II, xxvi, 757, and xxvii, 759. [2] II, xxix, 762. [3] II, xxxii, 766–768.
[4] II, xxx, 763. The collection was already in vogue in the Empire, but the State took the money. For a previous attempt on a universal scale *cf.* the transactions at the Council of Bourges, 1226 (*Chron. Rogeri de Wendover*, Rolls Ser., ii, 302).
[5] II, xviii, 741–742. [6] II, xxxiii, 768–769.

NICOLAS OF CUSA

The " King of the Romans " is superior to other kings, just
as the Pope is to his patriarchs.   He is independent of the
spiritual power and must not interfere in episcopal or
pontifical elections; there must be no encroachment of
the temporal upon the spiritual sphere or *vice versa*; and
in this connexion he attacks the theory of the *translatio
imperii* and demolishes the myth of the Donation of Con-
stantine.[1]   Yet the Emperor is not unconcerned with the
Church, for he is the defender of the orthodoxy taught by
the clergy, and, just as kings convoke national councils for
the reform of abuses within their domain, so the Emperor
should perform that function for the Universal Church,
if the Pope omits to do so; and in an assembly so con-
voked it will be his duty to preside and to labour for the
submission of those who resist its decrees.[2]   Here Nicolas
is thinking of the Emperor Sigismund and the Hussites
summoned to Basel in 1433.   He then proceeds to discuss
reform within the Empire, and in striking phrases pictures
its decadence.   Spiritual possessions have been absorbed
by the temporal power.[3]   The Emperor is often the creature
of the electors.[4]   Justice is set at naught, for the feudal
defiance or *diffidatio* is used to cover naked declarations of
war for selfish ends.[5]   " Mortal disease has invaded the
Germanic Empire.   Unless salutary aid is quickly given
death will undoubtedly follow, and the Empire will be
sought in Germany and shall not be found there." [6]   It
was true.   The stranger was at the gates.   Slavs in the
East, Burgundians in the West, were rolling back the
Empire from the territories it had won.   The defence desired by the princes was a loose federal autonomy under the

[1] III, ii, 782–783.   He says he can find no warrant for it in history;
but, characteristically, he adds : " Salvo in omnibus iudicio sacræ Synodi."
That a mediæval German should find no evidence for the *translatio imperii
de Græcis in Germanos* shows a critical spirit.

[2] III, xiv, 796; xxiv, 808.   [3] III, xxix, 812.   [4] III, xxx, 812.
[5] III, xxxi, 813.   [6] III, xxxi, 813 and 814.

47

purely nominal authority of the Emperor; the plan of the Emperors was far greater centralisation. In a way the problem was analogous to that which beset the Church. Here again, just as he had wished to safeguard the authority of the Pope and of the Council alike, so Nicolas desired to find a middle term between Imperial absolutism and the rights of the princes—to reconcile the principle of monarchy with that of federalism.[1] His first proposal was a general diet to be held annually at Frankfurt in order to maintain the safety of the Empire and to provide for the judicial reform so urgently needed. For this he proposed a division of the Empire into twelve districts, in each of which should sit an Imperial tribunal of three judges, a noble, an ecclesiastic, and a *bourgeois*, whose judgments the executive authority of the Emperor would carry out. The same diet must undertake the reform of taxation, and the simplification of law and custom.[2] There must be a new method of electing the Emperor;[3] he must be supported by a sufficient army maintained at public expense, for lawlessness must be put down with a vigorous hand.[4] The system of constant appeals from the secular power to the Roman Curia must be stopped.[5] Usury, gambling, luxury in clothing, must be suppressed.[6] But the return to severity and simplicity must be done gradually and with discretion. The Emperor has to act the part of the lyre-player; the laws are the strings of his lyre, and should not be stretched too tight, but all to the right and proportionate intervals, if harmony is to be achieved.[7]

[1] Vansteenberghe, *op. cit.*, p. 48.
[2] *De Conc. Cath.*, III, xxxv, 814–815.
[3] The plan is worked out in III, xxxvii, 817. See the discussion by Scharpff, *Der Cardinal und Bischof Nicolaus von Cues*, pp. 84–89.
[4] III, xxxix, 819–820.   [5] III, xl, 820.   [6] III, xl, 821.
[7] III, xli, 824 : " Debet itaque citharœdus rex esse ; et qui bene sciat in fidibus concordiam observare tam maiores quam minores, nec nimis nec minus extendere ut communis concordantia per omnium harmoniam resonet." Nothing has been said here of the treatise written by Nicolas shortly after

It is a fundamental characteristic of mediæval political thought that it refuses to be troubled by the discrepancy between idea and fact. If a divided and distracted Europe cannot realise the idea of unity in practice, it is the fault of man's mortal nature; the idea stands immutable, unshaken by human experience. It is itself the reality, human polity but the shadow, the inevitably poor attempt at reproduction. Nicolas accepted the idea, and did his best to better the earthly counterpart; his was not the positive Renaissance mind in politics, that dethrones the idea, whatever philosophy may say, as soon as pragmatical tests have proved it unsatisfying. There were Renaissance minds all around. What disillusionment, then, was in store for the author of this calm mediæval liberalism![1] A monument to the ideal of an organically harmonious Christendom, multiple in function, one in spirit, the treatise towers above the ambitions and antagonisms which it was powerless to reconcile. We must pass from the cool of the Spanish Chapel into the glare and noise of the *piazza* outside.

Within four years the author was on the side of Eugenius. He had resigned his position as a judge on the Commission of the Faith which was preparing the extreme measures against the Pope decided upon in 1436 by a majority of the Council: and he had been to Constantinople as a delegate of the papalist minority to urge the claims of an Italian city for the meeting-place of the coming Council between Greeks and Latins, as against Avignon, the choice of the

the *De Concordantia Catholica* entitled *Tractatus de Auctoritate Præsidendi in Concilio Generali*, printed in Dux, *Der deutsche Cardinal Nicolaus von Cues*, I Band, Beilage 1, pp. 475–491. Of this Scharpff remarks (*op. cit.*, p. 66) that it reveals no new standpoint.

[1] " Its sweet reasonableness of tone, its lofty eloquence, the sanctified common sense, which refuse to allow the absolute claims of legal rights upon a society which needs renovation, suggest a comparison with Hooker, to whose theory of law that of Nicolas bears a strong resemblance " (Figgis, *op. cit.*, p. 70).

majority. The transition is startling, but should not be set down to pure self-interest. Nicolas had, it is true, lost the case which he had originally come to Basel to advocate— that of Ulrich of Manderscheid suing for the archbishopric of Cologne against the papal nominee, Rabanus of Helmstadt—and the defeat may have made him disillusioned with the assembly; he may, perhaps, have been tempted by the promises of a well-known humanist, Ambrogio Traversari, who was at Basel in October 1435 by order of Eugenius on propaganda work; but a more powerful motive must have been the fact that in 1434–5 the Council was attempting, with little or no administrative experience, and no realisation of the difficulties, to grasp the whole machinery of the Church, judicial, executive, and legislative, and was being led on, largely by the French radicals, to extreme courses without realising the consequences.[1] Nicolas was the very opposite of a revolutionary.[2] The reform which he passionately desired was dependent on concord and could not be achieved by the more drastic methods of Cardinal Aleman; and it is not surprising that when his delicately adjusted constitutional scheme gained no permanent attention he transferred his allegiance to the side of a bureaucracy which at least had the merit of being efficient, fully awake to the evils in the Church, humanist and enlightened, and chose the narrower and more effective method by which to try to bring his own country to reform.

---

[1] There is plentiful evidence of the extended activities of the Council in the notaries' manuals published by J. Haller, *Concilium Basiliense: Studien und Quellen*, vol. iii, *Die Protokolle des Concils 1434–5*, which show its enormous agenda from day to day.

[2] Scharpff's characterisation of the purpose of *De Concordantia Catholica* is apposite here (*op. cit.*, pp. 70, 71): " Cusa war kein Stürmer in der Kirche; der Begriff von Reformation der Kirche, den das sechszehnte Jahrhundert aufstellte, war ihm ganz und gar fremd; sein Ziel war, die Kirche auf die geläutete durch Kirchengesetze geregelte Form, wie sie sich durch die Wirksamkeit der ersten acht allgemeinen Concilien gestallet hatte, zurückzuführen und bei allen Verbesserungen nicht beliebigen Eingebungen zu folgen, sondern ' die bewährten Pfäde der Väter einzuhalten.' "

NICOLAS OF CUSA

Looking back we might say that he chose the ideal of the ultramontane Papacy, the way of Antonelli rather than the way of Newman. Yet peace and unity were still to be his aim. The " Hercules of the Eugenians," as Æneas Silvius called him, was faithful to his mission of harmony.

He was first employed in helping Cardinal Carvajal to reclaim for St Peter his own Germany, which had declared its neutrality in the struggle of Pope and Council. Everywhere his arguments centred round the simple formula, " The Church is where there is unity, as at Ferrara and Florence, not where division exists, as at Basel." It is a little sad to think that not six years before he had argued for the Basel assembly on very similar grounds. His advocacy was eventually successful. By 1439 he had attached to the papal cause the electors of Cologne, Trier, Saxony, and the Palatinate, and finally in 1447 came the abolition of German neutrality and adhesion to Rome. For this he was rewarded by Nicholas V with the cardinalate of St Peter ad Vincula and the next year sent as legate *a latere* to Germany, to proclaim the indulgence of the Jubilee which the Pope was preparing and to carry out the practical reforming aims of his *Catholic Concord*. He was, his commission states, to establish social peace, redress doctrinal error, and correct moral abuses, by means of provincial councils, visitations of monastic houses, preaching, and the exercise of special judicial powers. All this he did with immense energy. For peace he strove by reconciling episcopal and capitular authorities in various places, by composing the quarrels of regulars and seculars, by smoothing down the differences between the clergy and the communes; and, while strengthening and safeguarding the powers of the bishops, he took good care to supervise and regulate the duties of their extremely unpopular henchmen, the archdeacons. He laboured vigorously for reform in

51

the monasteries: how difficult this was in actual practice, how stiff the obstacles put in the way of his decrees, can be gauged from the opposition offered to his reforming efforts by the Abbess Verena of the Sonneburg, whose bitter obstinacy was supported by Duke Sigismund of Austria, Count of the Tyrol. If Louis XI has been called the great spider spinning its web in the centre of the Christian world, the Count of the Tyrol may be represented as one of many little spiders spinning their webs in the centre of the Empire. With him Nicolas was to come into still more acute conflict when in 1453 he took up the bishopric which he was to hold for the rest of his life.

That year he was given the see of Brixen by Pius II, the famous Æneas Silvius Piccolomini, who had known him well at Basel and had remained on the Conciliar side some time after Nicolas' change of front. The appointment was not to Duke Sigismund's taste. The Count of the Tyrol was seeking to enlarge his frontier at the expense of the bishoprics of Trent, Chur, and Brixen. On the vacancy of the latter see the chapter had elected a compliant tool, John Roettel, and the nomination of the ardent reformer appeared likely to frustrate his plans. He was determined to exact fealty from the newcomer: the new bishop was equally determined to hold his diocese as a principality. With the exception of a few periods of *détente* or intervals when Nicolas was helping the Pope in the reform and management of the Patrimony, there was steadily increasing friction between count and cardinal for ten years, and in the end open warfare, league and counter-league, while the prestige of the Church in Southern Germany suffered not a little through the malicious appeals to German patriotism and anti-clerical sentiment spread by Gregory of Heimburg, the able and bitter lawyer and opponent of Nicolas, in the employment of Sigismund. It is a melancholy

NICOLAS OF CUSA

story. Naked acquisitiveness fought stubborn and pedantic legalism, for the peacemaking prelate cannot be acquitted of acts that were both provocative and tactless. Near the middle of the struggle he tired, wished to withdraw, but Pius was determined to make the affair of Brixen a test case. The Curia fought Heimburg for the temporal power and fought him over the author of the *Catholic Concord*. Once more Conciliar pamphleteering and propaganda, insolent appeals to the princes of the Empire, and placards of *gravamina* made their appearance. Only Sigismund's death (1463) stopped the campaign, and neither Nicolas nor his master lived longer than a year to enjoy a doubtful triumph.

Yet it is to these later years that some of the cardinal's best work, whether in mathematics, philosophy, or devotional writing, is to be attributed. During serene intervals in the tiresome bickering with Sigismund he was pondering deeply the problem of religious unity. If truth or reality is one, the good one, God Himself one, and men, as he held, striving to become partakers in that single good, why are there so many dissensions about the way that leads thither, and why are religions, whose only aim is to point out that way, at continual strife with one another ? Not only the dissensions in the Christian body itself, as, for example, the Hussite intransigeance, but the still more disastrous clash of East and West in the fall of Constantinople and the atrocities committed there by the Turks set him to think over the question. In September 1453 he tells us that after prolonged meditation he had a vision, in which he saw how the differences of the warring sects were permanently reconciled in a vast system of religious unity. The account of it he gives in the most imaginative and literary of his works, the *De Pace Fidei*, which reads like an epilogue to the *Catholic Concord*. If it were not in

53

dialogue form it would resemble a Platonic myth, where truth apprehended intuitively is set out in the graceful language of allegory. Olympus might almost be the scene, but the air is kindlier. The King of Heaven has just announced above the sad news which He has received from the earth. The angels of the different provinces and sects, whom He sent into the world, appear before the assembly of the elect and supplicate for mercy and compassion on humanity. "Thou, Lord, hast been pleased to create man of the clay of the earth and hast breathed into him a rational spirit that in him may shine the image of Thine ineffable virtue; and though that spirit of understanding which Thou didst sow in the earth hath been dimmed and seeth not the light nor whence it arose, yet Thou hast created for him all things that stir his senses to wonder, that he may be able some time to lift the eyes of his mind to Thee, creator of all, and to be united to Thee in deepest love, and so at last return with profit to the source of his being." But, continues the speaker, man has multiplied, and with great numbers has come great diversity: almost all men have to lead a miserable and laborious existence; few have the leisure to use their judgment so as to know and seek after God. "Thus Thou has sent unto Thy people kings and seers called prophets to teach them in Thy name worship and laws, which they have accepted as if from Thee : to the different nations Thou hast sent different prophets and teachers, now at one time, now at another. But the conditions of human life are such that long custom which has passed into habit is defended as truth. Thus have arisen no small dissensions when each community prefers its own faith to that of others. To our help, therefore, Thou that alone canst ! For 'tis on Thy account, whom alone they venerate, that there is this rivalry in their adoration. For no one, in aught that he

54

seemeth to seek, seeketh but the Good which is Thee. No
one in any quest of the mind followeth but the Truth which
Thou art. What asketh the living but to live, the existing
but to exist ? Thou art the giver of life and existence, and
it is Thou, it seems, that art sought in different ways
through different rites and art called by different names
because Thou remainest for all unknown, never to be
defined. Hide not Thyself, then, Lord : show Thy face,
and all people will be saved . . . for if Thou shalt do this the
sword and hatred shall cease and every ill, and all shall know
that there is but one religion in the multiplicity of rites."[1]
The King then speaks : He has given men free will, He
has sent them the prophets, and finally He sent them the
Word. What more could He do ? But the Word made
flesh takes up the plea. Although the Father's works are
perfect, yet because of the gift of free will and the fact that
there is nothing stable in this world of sense, that opinions,
conjectures, and interpretations are manifold, let the diversity of religions be brought to one orthodox faith.[2] The
Father assents. Wise men are accordingly summoned
from every nation who discuss with the Word, St Peter,
and St Paul the difficulties which will be met with in bringing their respective sects and countries to the unity of the
faith. A series of brilliant dialogues follows, which show
that Nicolas was more than a superficial student of comparative religion and of national modes of belief. A Greek,
an Italian, a Hindu, an Arab, a Chaldean, a Jew, a Scythian,
a Persian, a Syrian, a Spaniard, a Tartar, a German, a
Bohemian, and finally an Englishman appear (Pagan and
Christian are jumbled up in a remarkable order) and raise
difficulties which are satisfactorily answered, though some
accept the replies with rather unconvincing readiness. The
Arab asks how the polytheists are to be convinced, and

[1] i, 862–863.   [2] iii, 863–864.

receives the answer that even they assume the existence of
Deity, which they honour implicitly in their various gods
and which they recognise as the first principle of the universe.[1] The Hindu asks what is to happen to the idols,
and when he is told that they must be broken answers that
people believe in them because of the replies which they
give. He is informed, somewhat ingenuously, that the
oracle is usually given by the priest, and when this is
known the people will not want idols.[2] The Chaldean
asks if by the Trinity is meant a God only metaphorically
speaking three, for like the Arab he cannot understand how
God can have a Son.[3] The Frenchman acutely asks how
the differences of opinion on the purpose of the Incarnation
can be reconciled:[4] the Armenian raises difficulties over
baptism,[5] the Bohemian (as no doubt he would) over
the Eucharist,[6] and the Englishman, no ritualist, asks if
other sacraments—marriage, ordination, confirmation, and
extreme unction—will be insisted on. He receives from
St Paul the wise and truly Catholic answer that allowances
will be made for the weakness of men unless it goes against
their eternal safety. All nations will not be compelled to
accept the *régime* of fastings and abstentions: *augebitur
etiam fortassis devotio ex quadam diversitate.*[7] Perhaps St
Peter might have answered differently. Finally the wise
men are sent back to bring their countries to the unity of
the true religion and to attend as plenipotentiaries at Jerusalem, the " common centre," and there make perpetual
peace.

The enlightened theism, the strongly unecclesiastical
character of the vision, may appear a little strange in the
writer of the Letters to the Bohemians, in so prominent an
ecclesiastical statesman. But it is in fact the inevitable

[1] vi, 865–866. [2] vii, 866. [3] viii, 867. [4] xi, 869.
[5] xvi, 877. [6] xvii, 877. [7] xviii, 878.

outcome of his philosophy. Its characteristic is its relativism. No single philosophical system can truly answer the question what God is, what His relation to the cosmos, why and how the world was created. Each system possesses a certain degree of truth, but each by itself is fundamentally " conjecture." Only through a study of the various systems can one have an inkling of " the unity of the unattainable truth." [1] They participate in that truth, but not all equally ; the criterion lies in their theories of knowledge—their epistemologies, as we might call it. What then constitutes a probable theory of knowledge ? Here we touch the keynote of his thought : a theory, he would reply, that is ready to rely on intuition, which can surmount or, more accurately, combine contradictions, rather than on reason, which boggles at them. As early as 1440, in his *De Docta Ignorantia*, Nicolas stated the position which he was consistently to uphold throughout his philosophical writing : " The principle of contradiction is valid only for our reason." [2] He distinguishes fundamentally between the discursive reason, the *ratio discurrens*, which cannot admit the unity of opposites, and the intuitive vision, the *intellectus videns*, which perceives and admits it. [3] True and perfect knowledge is the knowledge which comes from the luminous insight of the *intellectus*. And why not from the reason ? Reality (*veritas*) Nicolas understands in the metaphysical sense of ' being,' making the two terms, as the scholastic philosophers did, interchangeable—*ens et verum convertuntur*; but as a Platonist he thinks of reality as God, in Whom all things are but participations. Reality for him

---

[1] *De Coniecturis*, I, ii, 76 : " Cognoscitur igitur inattingibilis veritatis unitas alteritate coniecturali."

[2] " Tout Hegel n'est-il pas en germe dans cette affirmation, et le seul fait de l'avoir formulée ne fait-il pas de Nicolas de Cues un des pères de la pensée allemande ? " (Vansteenberghe, *op. cit.*, p. 282).

[3] The whole of the *Apologia Doctæ Ignorantiæ*, pp. 63–75, especially p. 72, deals with this vital matter.

is not such and such a being, but infinite Being, unique, indivisible—God. But God, the *nomen maximum*, is above all understanding : how then can the reason understand things in their essence? Then again, on Aristotle's definition, true knowledge is knowledge *per causas*; but the first cause is God, and knowledge to be perfect must include a knowledge of His infinite Being. Reason is inadequate here : the end of knowledge is hidden in God.[1] Now reality is one, indivisible, without contrarieties ; the principle of contradiction along which reason works will not let reason consider it in its infinite simplicity. But the understanding—the *intellectus*—can lift itself to that height. " It should be the profound effort of our whole mental nature to raise itself to that simplicity where contradictories coincide." [2] The reconciliation not only of metaphysical but also of political and religious antagonisms is attainable by the inward eye of vision. Within the systematic unity that is God the opposites are comprised.

The *coincidentia oppositorum* is the main preoccupation of this remarkable man's thought. It was unfolded in a subtle and profound system of philosophy, illustrated throughout by geometrical diagrams and elaborated with a mathematician's care ; it was shot with a mystic's emotion and made high and holy with the devotion of a lofty spirit. But the politicians of the city-state and the Curia were to take little account of so transcendent a structure. There could be no concord when the invader came over the Alpine passes, or the galleys of Spain set out upon the unharvested sea, or the trumpet of a prophecy was blown at Wittenberg. Yet the constitutional doctrine which was its outcome is

---

[1] *Apologia Doctæ Ignorantiæ*, p. 64 : "Nichil perfecte homo scire poterit: finis enim scientiæ in Deo reconditus est."
[2] *De Docta Ignorantia*, III, xii, 62 : "Debet autem in his profundus omnis nostri humani ingenii conatus esse, ut ad illam se elevet simplicitatem, ubi contradictoria coincidunt."

part of the legacy of the Middle Ages to the political thought of the West ; it was to be listened to again in its calm essential reasonableness, when the absolutist ideals of territorial rulers provoked their reaction. The forms of political organisation which it advocated soon died out of men's thoughts ; but its spiritual core, consent and representation, compromise without extremities, unity through the conference board, is being fought for still.

E. F. JACOB

BIBLIOGRAPHY

For a list of Nicolas of Cusa's writings and a bibliography of general editions of his works and of monographs and articles upon his life and works see E. Vansteenberghe, *Le Cardinal Nicolas de Cues*, pp. 465–490, and ix–xvii. The literature is large, and only a small selection can be given here.

A. PRIMARY SOURCES (PRINTED)

Collected works : (i) Ed. Jacques Lefèvre. Paris, 1514.
             (ii) Ed. Petri. Basel, 1565.
Special editions : *De Auctoritate Præsidendi in Concilio Generali*, in J.M. Dux, *Der deutsche Cardinal Nicolaus von Cues und die Kirche seiner Zeit*. 2 vols. Regensburg, 1847.
    Reformatio Generalis. Ed. Ehses, in *Historisches Jahrbuch*, t. xxxii, pp. 281–297.
    De Docta Ignorantia. Ed. P. Rotta. Bari, 1913.

B. MONOGRAPHS AND ARTICLES

(a) General Biography

DUX, J. M., and E. VANSTEENBERGHE, *ut supra*.
EUCKEN, R. : " Nicolaus von Cues," in *Philosophische Monatshefte*, t. xiv. 1878.
FUNK, V. : " Nicolaus von Cues," in *Kirchenlexicon*, 2nd ed., t. ix. 1895.
LONG, P. : " Nicolas de Cuse," in *Encylopédie des sciences religieuses* (ed. Lichtenberger), t. ix. 1880.
MORIN, F. : " Nicolas de Cues," in *Dictionnaire de théologie scolastique*. 1856–65.

59

RENAISSANCE AND REFORMATION THINKERS

PRANTL, G. VON : " Nicolaus v. Cues," in *Allgemeine deutsche Biographie*, t. iv. 1876.

SCHARPFF, FR. A. : *Der Cardinal und Bischof Nicolaus von Cues als Reformator in Kirche, Reich und Philosophie.* 1871.

SCHMID, R. : " Cusanus," in *Realencyclopädie für protestantische Theologie und Kirche*, t. iv. 1898.

(b) Special Studies

DUHEM, P. : " Nicolas de Cues et Léonard de Vinci," in *Léonard de Vinci*, t. ii. 1909.

FALCKENBERG, R. : *Grundzüge der Philosophie des Nic. Cusanus mit besonderer Berucksichtigung der Lehre vom Erkennen.* 1880.

MARX, J. : *Nikolaus von Cues und seine Stiftungen zu Cues und Deventer.* 1906.

ROSSI, C. : *Niccolà di Cusa e la direzione monistica della filosofia nel rinascimento.* 1893.

STUMPF, R. : *Die politischen Ideen des Nicolaus von Cusa.* 1865.

UEBINGER, JOH. : *Die Gotteslehre des Nicolaus Cusanus.* 1888.

C. GENERAL WORKS ON THE PERIOD

CREIGHTON, MANDELL : *History of the Papacy during the Reformation*, vols. i and ii. 1892.

FIGGIS, J. N. : *From Gerson to Grotius.* 1916.

HALLER, JOH. : *Concilium Basiliense : Studien und Quellen zur Geschichte des Concils von Basel.* 4 vols. 1896–1903.

PASTOR, L. : *History of the Popes*, vols. i–iii (Eng. translation).

PÉROUSE, C. : *Le Cardinal Louis Aleman et la fin du Grand Schisme.* 1904.

VALOIS, NOEL : *Le Pape et le Concile* (1418–1450). 2 vols. 1909.

VOIGT, A. : *Enea Silvio de' Piccolomini als Papst Pius II und sein Zeitalter.* 3 vols. 1851–63.

III

SIR JOHN FORTESCUE

IT is difficult for the average Englishman to think of, or even to remember, the Renaissance as a great land-mark or watershed in our history. Our thought turns naturally to literature rather than to any of the other arts, and we think, whether rightly or wrongly, of literature as a purely native product. The earliest poet we really know—Chaucer—gives us a gallery of brilliant figures, clad, it is true, in mediæval garb, but alive and real as we are to-day, and endowed with that peculiar sense of humour, that gift of humorous understatement, which bridges the centuries and even the oceans.

We cannot class Chaucer as pre-Renaissance any more than we can naturally describe Marlowe or Spenser or Shakespeare as post-Renaissance. The labels are meaning-less. The contrasted names merely remind us of the steady familiar growth of England.

Yet in this list of lectures on political thinkers of the Renaissance we find two Englishmen, Sir John Fortescue and Sir Thomas More. Of these, Sir Thomas More almost gives the lie to what I have said above; he stands in the direct line of Greek and Italian influences; he *is* the Classical Renaissance in England. Nevertheless, he would never have grudged an evening spent at supper with Chaucer, and Shakespeare, if not Marlowe, might have strolled in the garden with him at Chelsea.

Fortescue is a different matter. He is the most out-standing and original political writer in England in the fifteenth century. That is his claim to stand in this group. What then does he represent? Is he a mediæval writer or a modern? What has he to teach, and where did he learn it? Is he a purely native product, or did he learn from years of exile to know the ferment of opinion that gathered around the Conciliar Movement and foretold the Renaissance?

His choice as a Renaissance type seems to need some word of justification.

One of the pleasantest of the minor diversions of historians is the habit of selecting national types on more or less paradoxical lines. It has been argued, in Oxford, that the four men really characteristic of England, who could have been produced or paralleled nowhere else, are Cædmon, Langland, Bunyan, and Cobbett—all men of letters, but humble men of small education. The more one thinks of it, the more the choice convicts one of truth.

Another line of choice would illustrate that specifically English gift of prosaic, semi-humorous understatement of the truth of which I have already spoken, sometimes used for the purpose of sober self-justification, sometimes with a hardly veiled wish to exasperate a high-flying opponent.

King Alfred's reason for his scanty legislative efforts is the earliest example I know. " It was not known to me which of these might seem good to them that come after." At the other end of long centuries is Burke: " I have taken my idea of Liberty very low, that it may stick to me to the end of my life," or Dr Johnson's " Every lover of Liberty stands doubtful of the fate of posterity, because the chief county in England cannot take its representative from a jail."

There are links all through the centuries, especially perhaps among the lawyers. " A king is a thing men have made for their own sakes, for quietness' sake, just as in one family one man is appointed to buy the meat. . . . If they have not what they would have one day, they shall have it the next, or something as good," says Selden. Only a shade more serious is the poet Marvell's pregnant and unequalled summing-up of the Great Civil War: " Methinks the cause too good to have been fought for."

It is to this line of Englishmen that Fortescue belongs, to this temperament that he is akin, though I am bound to admit that moderation is more marked than humour in his writings. If, then, Fortescue is a typical Englishman, in what sense was he a Renaissance thinker? Perhaps in the range rather than in the content of his thought.

Now the Renaissance in England meant many things. We often apologise for our English Renaissance. It needs no apology. It was classical, scholarly, and sane ; it was literary and exuberant, if a little belated. It did not burn lamps before the bust of Plato, but Colet saw to it that the children he loved so well learned both Greek and Christianity with less thrashing than ever before. It produced music that was unrivalled in Europe. Even in painting there were two strongly marked lines in which we may trace a real renaissance.

England had its vigorous aristocratic art, the art of patronage, of highly critical patrons, men who believed in the unknown painters of Richard II, in Holbein, in Mabuse, in Torrigiano the sculptor. Moreover, England had also a vigorous popular art, an art which preserved for us the peasant types of East Anglia and of Kent, and which, right up to the Reformation, beautified life with embroidery, with illuminations, with stained glass, carved ivories, and all the many arts and crafts in which mediæval England had so widespread a reputation. Moreover, England developed Perpendicular architecture, letting in the light, and edifying the *bourgeois*.

Fortescue belongs essentially to the English rather than to the Continental Renaissance in the balance of his qualities and his interests, in his attachment to the things he knows, in his refusal to plunge; he represents that renaissance of the ordinary citizen, of middle-class culture, which owed so little to the recovery of Plato, to the conquest of Constantinople, or to any of the traditional causes of the Renaissance.

Biographically, Fortescue exactly represents the fifteenth century in England. He was probably born in 1400, or just before ; he died at some unknown date after 1476. He belonged to a Devon family, and may have been sent to Exeter College, Oxford. In any case, his education was mainly legal, at Lincoln's Inn. He has left us a famous description of life and study in the Inns of Court, too well known, Mr Plummer thought, to bear quotation. But I believe the repetition of one or two passages may be pardoned. Fortescue begins by explaining that there were at least ten lesser inns, called Inns of Chancery, besides the four Inns of Court; the cost of living at one of these Inns he calculates at twenty-eight pounds a year; then he goes on:

> There is both in the Inns of Court, and the Inns of Chancery, a sort of an Academy, or Gymnasium, fit for persons of their station ; where they learn singing, and all kinds of music, dancing and such other accomplishments and diversions (which are called Revels) as are suitable to their quality, and such as are usually practised at Court. At other times, out of term, the greater part apply themselves to the study of the law. Upon festival days, and after the offices of the church are over, they employ themselves in the study of sacred and prophane history : here every thing which is good and virtuous is to be learned : all vice is discouraged and banished. So that knights, barons, and the greatest nobility of the kingdom, often place their children in those Inns of Court; not so much to make the laws their study, much less to live by the profession (having large patrimonies of their own), but to form their manners and to preserve them from the contagion of vice. The discipline is so excellent, that there is

scarce ever known to be any picques or differences, any bickerings or disturbances amongst them. The only way they have of punishing delinquents, is by expelling them the society ; which punishment they dread more than criminals do imprisonment and irons : for he who is expelled out of one society, is never taken in by any of the other. Whence it happens, that there is a constant harmony amongst them, the greatest friendship and a general freedom of conversation.

In another passage Fortescue would seem to admit that it is possible to work in term time :

Here, in Term-time, the students of the law attend in great numbers, as it were to public schools, and are there instructed in all sorts of Law-learning, and in the practice of the Courts ; the situation of the place, where they reside and study, is between Westminster and the city of London, which, as to all necessaries and conveniences of life, is best supplied of any city or town in the kingdom ; the place of study is not in the heart of the city itself, where the great confluence and multitude of the inhabitants might disturb them in their studies ; but, in a private place, separate and distinct by itself, in the suburbs, near to the Courts of Justice aforesaid, that the students, at their leisure, may daily and duly attend with the greatest ease and convenience.

Fortescue's legal life is tolerably easy to trace, and there are records of his gradual acquisition of property in various western counties, including the Manor of Ebrington, just east of Chipping Campden, where he is buried.

The most vivid picture of a barrister's life in the fifteenth century is to be found in the Paston Letters. It was a life alternating between rustic peace on one of his country estates, superintending the harvest operations ; periods of travel and discomfort on circuit ; and the ordinary law-terms in town, when the separation from his wife entailed a fairly frequent correspondence, in which she recorded the despatch of rabbits for his larder, and he explained why he could not carry out, with any precision, her directions

65

as to the purchase of dress materials. There are none of Fortescue's letters extant, and one gathers an impression that they would have been less lively than those of John and Margaret Paston, perhaps also less full of strife and litigation. But the general plan of life must have been much the same.

By 1440 Fortescue was a Judge of Assize in Norfolk; in 1441 he was made a King's Sergeant, an office which brought him into close contact with the Council. In 1442 he was a Chief Justice of the King's Bench, and he was knighted in the following year.

From this time forward the fortunes of Fortescue are closely intertwined with those of the house of Lancaster, and it is impossible to follow them in detail. He was brought into close relations with the Council, with practical difficulties of administration, with popular risings, with problems of the royal succession, with the problem of the proper function of monarchy—and that too at a time when the King was a saint of the second class, a saint whose withdrawal from the world never issued, as with St Louis, or St Catherine of Siena, in an increased ability to deal with the worldly problems to which they returned.

After 1460 Fortescue was constantly on the Continent in attendance on the exiled royal family, in Flanders, Burgundy, and Paris. After 1471 came a reconciliation with the Yorkists, the motives and explanation of which are not very clear. Apparently his work *In Praise of the Laws of England* was written for the edification of the young Prince Edward, while it is not clear whether his *Monarchia, or Governance of England* was originally intended to embody the praise of Henry VI or of Edward IV. Mr Plummer inclines to the latter opinion.

It is perhaps characteristically English that it is such a man of affairs, after such a busy practical life, who writes the political theory of the English Constitution as he saw it in the fifteenth century, and as it was seen again by most of the "constitutional rebels" of the early seventeenth century.

The age itself demands a word. Stubbs has described the fifteenth century as futile, bloody, and immoral—more futile, bloody, and immoral than the fourteenth. Yet at least it saw one great development, in which England shared to the full. It was the age in which national languages fought their last fight and conquered; the age of a final general use of the vernacular tongue for all kinds of purposes. Miss M. Deanesly[1] has recently traced in connexion with the "Lollard Bible" the general European demand for the vernacular Scriptures—a demand which was largely an outgrowth of the semi-secular religious life which was becoming almost more common than strict monasticism, as is witnessed by the numerous Third Orders, Brethren of the Common Life, Friends of God, and other loosely knit associations of mystics and ascetics. For the fifteenth century was not only the age of a commercial and financial religion; it was also marked by a great widening of the stream of mystical life and literature. The great English mystics, Walter Hilton, Julian of Norwich, Richard Rolle, and the author of *The Cloud of Unknowing* had already, before its opening, entered upon their heritage of "English undefiled," alongside of Chaucer and Langland.

Following close upon the mystics, Reginald Pecock, best known by the attractive title of his chief work, *The Repressor of Over-much Blaming of the Clergy*, succeeded in bringing the theology and philosophy of Aquinas into the range of secular readers by writing in English; his temerity in making the attempt was perhaps his worst unorthodoxy, yet he suffered the fate of a heretic.

So with Fortescue. In many respects he was still mediæval, adding little to Aristotle, to Aquinas, or to Aquinas' *continuator*, the author of the *De Regimine Principum*.

[1] In *The Lollard Bible* (1920).

67

He is rather the typical Englishman living at the time of the Renaissance than a typical thinker of the Renaissance. Yet by writing his last summary of political thought, the *Governance of England*, in English, he fell into line with the great development of the century, and takes his place in the natural march of progress in England. He writes for the average citizen, for the man in the street. He might perhaps have used the politer, almost more natural, medium of French, but his residence abroad had convinced him that the French had corrupted their own tongue, which was now, he said, barely intelligible to men who knew the purer French of the English law-courts !

Fortescue was less original than Wycliffe in many ways. Yet in others he seems far ahead of his own days, and he makes a natural bridge between centuries. In some respects he is the forerunner of Montesquieu and of Bentham, and with close affinities to Burke. He thinks out the relationship between law and economic and social conditions, and between law and the Constitution. Seeing that a good system of law—far better than the civil law of the Romans, in his opinion—will not avail to avert disaster, he turns to the executive as the key to the position. To him, as to every other reformer of administrative methods, the question is how to secure an expert body of advisers, small enough to be efficient. His dream of a professional Council of twenty-four persons duly qualified for service in Church and State is not too unlike Temple's scheme two centuries later. In the end the problem of an effective Cabinet has always solved itself, silently and as if by chance. Fortescue stood at the beginning of a long series of schemes and attempts.

There are three main works of Fortescue which call for some detailed treatment—the *De Natura Legis Naturæ*, the *De Laudibus Legum Angliæ*, and the *Monarchia, or Governance of England*.

The *De Natura Legis Naturæ*, the earliest of Fortescue's works, is interesting as containing the outline of his political theory; he explores both the nature and the origin of monarchy, and of the royal authority, and his conclusions embody a characteristic compromise between old and new, mediæval and modern.

St Thomas (or rather, the pseudo-Aquinas, as Mr Plummer calls him) had believed that absolute monarchy, *dominium regale*, was likest God's authority, and therefore the nearest approach to perfection; although he admitted that a polity or a politic monarchy, *dominium politicum*, was better than tyranny, the rule of a bad king.

Fortescue adds to these alternatives a third category— a kingdom both politic and royal—*dominium politicum et regale*. This kingdom he finds actually existing: "For in the kingdom of England the kings make not laws, nor impose subsidies upon their subjects, without the consent of the three estates of the Realm. Nay, even the Judges of that kingdom are all bound by their oaths not to render judgment against the laws of the land, although they should have the command of the sovereign to the contrary."

These are the three tests of conditions of a "politic kingdom" to which Fortescue remains firm throughout his writings. But he admits that a politic king must on occasion rule royally; that is, he must have an emergency power. Equity also must be left to his sagacity. He departs from one of the classical mediæval doctrines by arguing that the State is not an evil in itself, and that the earliest ages were not golden. His picture of primitive society might well have inspired Hobbes, to whom the life of man in a state of nature was "solitary, poor, nasty, brutish, and short." Fortescue declares that "the pride of Nimrod first usurped dominion over men, and yet nothing better or more convenient than these things could have befallen the human race, inasmuch as if all things had remained common as before, and there had been no dominion over men upon earth, public affairs after men's sin would have been managed very ill for man, and for want of justice the human race would have torn itself to pieces in mutual slaughter." He quotes with approval the Aristotelian doctrine that man is by nature a social and political animal, and he ingeniously combines the two views of the origin of the State : "Thus did kingly supremacy get its origin and being, although under or from unbelievers, yet naturally and by the institution of Nature's Law." The law of nations he defines to be certain of the laws of nature which the nations have adopted which were so convenient for them that without them they could not live rightly.

The second part of the treatise is a technical discussion of the laws of succession, which takes the form of a highly anti-feminist manifesto, with arguments of this kind—in the form of a dialogue:

"Who ever hunts hares with cats? Nature disposes greyhounds for the fields and the pursuit of hares, but cats for staying at home to catch mice. It is a shame . . . to draw away from home for the purpose of governing nations, the woman whom nature has fitted for domestic duties." Fortescue would have objected to both Queen Elizabeth and Queen Victoria, but chiefly perhaps to the latter !

The lady of the dialogue replies at last : " . . . I do not, as my Uncle supposes, consider him to have given a satisfactory answer by his reasons to the points which he has stated ; nevertheless . . . fearing lest his gravity be tired out by a further lengthening of this argument, I do not intend to make any further reply."

Mr Plummer remarks that this work lacks the primary condition of success, namely, readableness!

The *De Laudibus Legum Angliæ* was written some years later, in a far less pedantic and academic style, though still in Latin. Fortescue had advanced beyond merely repeating the old formula, *Nolumus leges Angliæ mutare*; he was prepared to defend his opinion by a reasoned defence of English law as against the civil law. It is curious that Maitland seems to have interested himself so little in Fortescue. In his Rede Lecture on *English Law and the Renaissance* he discusses at length the apparent prospect of a "reception" of Roman law in England during the sixteenth century, parallel to the reception which formed the third *R* in German history. Yet he never mentions the fact—possibly because it was so familiar to him—that Fortescue had foreseen the possibility of such a reception in England and had fully discussed it, and rejected it, before 1470. Moreover, Fortescue had suggested the very reason which Maitland adduces for the survival of English law—the excellence of the organisation and the teaching in the Inns of Court. Maitland says, it may be remembered, "We may well doubt whether aught else could have saved English law in the age of the Renaissance."

The *Praise of the Laws of England* is written in the form of a dialogue between an aged Chancellor and a young Prince. It therefore forms a treatise on the duty and business of a prince, comparable in part with Machiavelli's *The Prince*, or with James I's *Basilicon Doron*. An Englishman would be apt to say that it compares very favourably with either. It provides a perfect storehouse of maxims which the lawyers were not slow to use against the Stuarts. The Chancellor begins by exhorting the Prince to study the laws, as he had studied martial exercises, for the sake of his people; the Prince retorts with a mild objection that

71

although he admits that Deuteronomy contains a law of divine institution, " yet the law to the study whereof you now invite me is merely human, derived from human authority." The Chancellor then defines his position clearly : " Be pleased to know then, that not only the Deuteronomical, but also all human laws are sacred, the definition of the law being this : ' It is a holy sanction, commanding whatever is honest, and forbidding the contrary.' And that must needs be holy which is so in its definition."

The great reason for the study of the law, the Chancellor goes on, is that the Prince may attain to felicity and happiness so far as possible in this life. Human laws are no other than rules whereby the perfect notion of justice can be determined—that justice which is virtue absolute and perfect, and therefore the *summum bonum* or beatitude, so that, having attained this justice, a man may be said to be made happy by the laws.

Another less exalted reason for studying the laws is that the Prince might be surprised and think them very queer, if he did not know them, whereas " Use becomes a second nature ! "

The Prince must study to acquire a habit of justice, a genuine reputation as a just prince, not merely an external reputation such as Machiavelli seems to advocate. Thereupon the Prince makes bold to ask which law he must study, and by what method. He is instructed, very firmly, that all he needs is a general knowledge of the principles of law, not the close study of twenty years which is necessary to make a judge—for the giving of judgments belongs to the judges, and not to the king. (Fortescue's attitude on this point may well be compared with the point of view of James I, both in his *Basilicon Doron* and also in his dealings with the judges.) The law which the Prince must study

72

is equally firmly laid down; excellent though the civil law may be, in those countries or states to which it belongs, yet the king of England *has no power to alter* the law of his kingdom, for a politic king cannot change the law but by the consent of the people. At this point Fortescue cautiously throws over Aristotle. His view stands in sharp contrast with that of Richard II, or Cardinal Pole,[1] or James I.

The intelligent young Prince now inquires why there are two kinds of kingdoms, absolute and politic; the Chancellor goes a stage farther than in the earlier treatise, and explains that absolute monarchy originates in conquest, while he quotes St Augustine to prove the origin of the politic kingdom in a pact, or consent of right, entered upon by the people for the sake of the common good. The nature of the State thus created is determined by the object and intention of the compact. In the body politic the first thing which lives and moves is " the intention of the people, having it in the blood, that is, the prudential care and provision for the public good, which it transmits . . . to the head as the principal part." The king " is appointed to protect his subjects in their lives, properties, and laws; for this very end and purpose he has the delegation of power from the people, and he has no just claim to any power but this." The body politic, thus formed, is a mystical body. Fortescue was in no danger of being led astray by his metaphor; he states clearly from the beginning what the ' organic ' view of society means to him.

The Chancellor goes on to treat of the statute law of England, having set aside the law of nature and custom. English statute law, he declares, is necessarily wise, since it is created by the consent of the whole kingdom. From this point onward he enters upon an elaborate comparison

[1] See Starkey's *Dialogue*.

between the civil law and the law of England, always greatly to the advantage of the latter. Into the technicalities of his argument it is not necessary to go farther. It is more to our purpose to note the points at which his outlook seems strikingly modern rather than typical of the Renaissance.

He admits, for example, that torture was used at times in England, but he adds : " For my own part, I see not how it is possible for the wound which such a judge [who permits torture] must give his own conscience, ever to close up or be healed ; as long, at least, as his memory serves him to reflect upon the bitter torture so unjustly and inhumanly inflicted on the innocent."

He is singularly modern, too, in his remark on the effect of torture upon the torturers : " The execution of the sentence of the law upon criminals is a task fit only for little villains [*ignobiles*] to perform, picked out from among the refuse of mankind." [1]   A probable miscarriage of justice, on circuit, haunted his memory for years.

Fortescue is very emphatic in his preference for a jury system above anything that the civil law could offer. Yet he saw clearly enough that there was no absolute perfection in the system, that it depended largely upon the existence of a stable, independent, and prosperous social order. It could not be transported into France. This argument gives occasion for a famous description of England's prosperity, which, rose-coloured though it be, bears yet a substantial testimony to the condition of the country. It is the more remarkable when we remember that Fortescue had just lived through the Wars of the Roses.

> England is a country so fertile, that, comparing it acre for acre, it gives place to no one other country : it almost produces things spontaneous, without man's labour or toil.   The fields, the plains,

---

[1] The apparent vigour of Fortescue's language owes much to his eighteenth-century translator.

groves, woodlands, all sorts of lands spring and prosper there so quick, they are so luxuriant, that even uncultivated spots of land often bring in more profit to the occupant than those which are manured and tilled ; though those too are very fruitful in plentiful crops of corn. The feeding lands are likewise enclosed with hedgerows and ditches, planted with trees which fence the herds and flocks from bleak winds and sultry heats, and are for the most part so well watered, that they do not want the attendance of the hind, either day or night. There are neither wolves, bears, nor lions in England ; the sheep lie out a nights without their shepherds, penned-up in folds, and the lands are improving at the same time ; whence it comes to pass, that the inhabitants are seldom fatigued with hard labour ; they lead a life more spiritual and refined.

. . . . . .

The inhabitants are rich in gold, silver, and in all the necessaries and conveniences of life. They drink no water, unless at certain times, upon a religious score, and by way of doing penance. They are fed, in great abundance, with all sorts of flesh and fish, of which they have plenty everywhere : they are clothed throughout in good woollens : their bedding and other furniture in their houses are of wool, and that in great store : they are also well provided with all other sorts of household goods and necessary implements for husbandry : every one, according to his rank, hath all things which conduce to make life easy and happy.

There are other interesting passages which illustrate the condition of the English law of bondage—of serfdom, or of slavery—during the fifteenth century, the period when serfdom, in fact, was rapidly disappearing. Fortescue has a habit of keeping close to the facts, of showing how economic facts and social conditions form the basis of law and legal principles; in this he belongs emphatically to the historical school of political thought, and would have delighted the heart of Bodin, of Montesquieu, of Burke. There is nothing ' high-flown ' about Sir John Fortescue.

The very natural question of the Prince as to why English law was not studied in the universities leads the Chancellor on to the quaint description of the Inns of Court, from which

75

I have already quoted. He gives much curious information about the Inns and their methods of procedure, and finally justifies even " the law's delay " by pointing out how much more convenient it is not to be hanged too promptly !

In the last chapter the Prince puts a characteristic gloss upon the saying of the doctors of the law : *"Imperator gerit omnia iura sua in scrinio pectoris sui. . . .* Not that he actually knows all the laws, but as he apprehends the principles of them, their method and nature, he may properly enough be said to understand them all." Fortescue's respect for the civil law, when combined with his regard for the English Constitution, seems almost to lead him into that perilous pastime known as running with the hare and hunting with the hounds. He reconciles the irreconcilable. On this note he ends what is probably the first work on comparative jurisprudence written in England, if not in Europe.

The *Monarchia, or Governance of England* is the latest of Fortescue's writings : it is written in English and is even more practical than the *Praise of the Laws,* and it approaches more nearly than either of his previous works the form and colour of a political pamphlet. In its practical suggestions, and its analysis of the present discontents, it is new ; in its political theory it merely repeats the principles of the two earlier treatises.

The author distinguishes once again the two kinds of kingdom, the *dominium regale* and the *dominium politicum et regale,* ignoring the *dominium politicum* of which he had previously written. He recapitulates his own description of their respective powers and their different origins; he argues once more that the absolute king possesses nothing which is not possessed by the politic king, save the power to do wrong. And this is really no added power : " To be able to sin is not power or liberty, no more than to be able to grow old or rotten."

From theory Fortescue turns to facts—the wealth or poverty of England or France, and the respective revenues of their kings. Poverty is the worst of sins in a king, for, as Aristotle said in the *Ethics*, " it is impossible for a poor man to do good works." Fortescue goes on to a close analysis of the king's ordinary and extraordinary charges, which throws interesting light upon the administration in the fifteenth century. The " king's charges " actually implies the whole public revenue, and hence under this head Fortescue is able to discuss the keeping of the Marches, or the need for a navy to keep off rovers, to protect merchants, and to save the country from invasion. The extraordinary charges differ little from the ordinary, save that they are irregular or unexpected. They imply the need for an emergency power, such as Fortescue had spoken of in the *De Natura Legis Naturæ*, when he declared that a politic king must sometimes act regally. A sudden invasion, for example, must be met out of the king's own coffers, before he can have any aid from his people. All this part of Fortescue's work is ostensibly practical, not theoretical—but occasionally a practical difficulty involves the definition of an abstract right.

The king's function may best be defined in borrowing the papal title *Servus servorum Dei*, but the people, in return, must remember that the labourer is worthy of his hire. This argument leads on, naturally enough, to the well-known description of the over-mighty subject, and the danger he may prove to the king. Fortescue is rather optimistic in his view of the motives behind this over-powerful rival : " Man's courage is so noble, that naturally he aspireth to high things." But Fortescue was apt to impute high motives ; even the multitude of thieves yearly hanged in England proves, not the dishonesty of the English nor the vigour of their judges, but only their high spirit, so infinitely greater than that of the French, of whom few indeed had spirit enough to steal, still less to be hanged for it! Fortescue's experiences in Scotland seem to have been impressive, for he asserts that there is no man hanged in Scotland in seven years for robbery; the hearts of Scotsmen will not serve them to go beyond larceny!

Fortescue also discusses the parallel question whether it was wise to keep the commons poor in order that they should be unable to rebel. He supplies two answers to his own question: first, England's strength lay in her archers, and if the class from which the archers were recruited was enfeebled by poverty the State would lose its best line of defence; secondly, poor men are always the most ready to risk a rising, " and thrifty men have been loath thereto, for dread of losing their goods." If they do join it is for fear that the poor will take their goods by force. Fortescue again insists on having the argument on his side, whatever the facts. Men will rise, he says, " for lack of goods, or for lack of justice. But certainly when they lack goods, they will rise, saying that they lack justice." Fortescue belongs to the group who, with Sully, believe that risings are caused by "*impatience de souffrir*," and not to those complacent followers of Hobbes, who believe that " men be most troublesome when they be most at ease." It is in this detailed social outlook that Fortescue is most in advance of his times, and yet his whole attitude is curiously unlike that of the typical Renaissance statesman.

The second main question in *The Governance of England* is the appointment and composition of the king's Council. This is a strictly practical question, in which Fortescue is drawing almost entirely upon experience, and finds little help in the scholastic authorities on politics. Indeed, the chapters which deal with this subject quote no authorities whatever, save the one maxim from the Gospels : " No man can serve two masters."

Fortescue's main objects in his reformation of the Council were, first, to obtain men devoted to the service of the State rather than to their own ends ; secondly, to obtain men who should be expert counsellors ; and, thirdly, to reduce the Council to a manageable size. His first scheme contemplates a body of thirty-two men, of whom twenty-four commoners are permanent councillors, and eight lords, spiritual and temporal, who change every year ; a second scheme proposes only twenty. Their work was to be partly administrative and partly deliberative, and they were to prepare legislative business for the Parliament and thereby save much valuable time.

Fortescue shows very clearly how well he understands the difficulty of securing an efficient, honest, and faithful executive ; he is laying down the lines on which first the Tudor Council, and secondly the modern Cabinet, have needed to be developed. He knows perfectly well that no politic king can keep the executive solely in his own hands, and he recognises that the traditional Council is out of date. Yet he is singularly cautious ; he never discusses the details of representative government, the limits of citizenship, or the methods by which consent might be given. He makes no use of the precedent of the minority of Henry VI, when the Council was chosen in Parliament. He is essentially not a theorist, but a man driven now and again to evolve a theory which should provide a permanent basis for his desired reforms. He prefers to speak about the case before him, rather than to judge abstract questions.

He seldom reaches any very high level of thought ; he

was a plain man, that loved his country. But that love was so strong that at last it roused him to eloquence. In what is essentially his last chapter (xx) he describes what great good will come of the firm endowing of the Crown—of a satisfactory provision for a revenue, as we should say. " The king who should make such an endowment shall do thereby daily more alms than shall be done by all the foundations that ever were made in England, and by reason of this foundation all men shall every day be the merryer, the surer, and shall fare the better in his body and all his goods. For this shall be a College in which shall sing and pray for evermore all the men of England spiritual and temporal." " We shall now," he concludes, " live under justice, which we have not done of long time, God knoweth."

The cobbler sticks to his last, even to the end, and the judge, who had troubled himself so often over the fate of the innocent, can only talk of politics or of religion in terms of justice. Practical though he was, he moved a little uneasily in an atmosphere of expediency. It is hardly possible to read Fortescue without seeking, at every turn, to remember some sharply contrasted dictum of Machiavelli.

It would be natural to seek further light upon Fortescue's personality in the fragmentary evidence of the Year-Books. If it has been possible to reconstruct the witty, irascible, homely temperament of Sir William Bereford, Chief Justice in Edward II's reign, surely a century later there should be signs of the character and influence of one of the greatest English judges. Lord Clermont, in the *Collected Works* of Fortescue, has brought together a large number of passages from the Year-books in which Fortescue's opinions or decisions are quoted. But they are singularly colourless ; nothing comparable to Bereford emerges. Fortescue remains, when one has gone through them, wise, measured, sensible, moderate, just, and even kindly, yet without

SIR JOHN FORTESCUE

humour. But the reader knows no more of Fortescue the man than before.[1]

The most famous legal question in which Fortescue was concerned was a matter of Parliamentary privilege— the lawfulness of Thorp's imprisonment, on which the Lords asked the judges for an opinion. The Chief Justice Fortescue, in the name of all the justices, after " sad communication and mature deliberation," answered and said " that they ought not to answer to that question; for it hath not been used aforetime that the justices should in any wise determine the privilege of the High Court of Parliament; for it is so high and so mighty in its nature that it may make law, and the determination and knowledge of that privilege belongeth to the Lords of the Parliament, and not to the justices."

The famous reply tells us little of Fortescue himself, but it is clear evidence of the critical times in which he lived, and the crucial questions of constitutional law and custom with which he was accustomed to deal. Parliament had secured its own existence in the fourteenth century; in the fifteenth century it had to adjust its claim to those of other members of the Constitution. There was much shaking down of ill bed-fellows to be done. Fortescue, who brought so little individual prejudice to his task, was peculiarly fitted to build up customs and principles that should endure.

It is open, I suppose, to a contributor to this book to attach each great thinker to the Renaissance or to the Reformation at choice. Fortescue lived in an age when religious changes were inevitably approaching, when sharp questionings were not to be abated by soft words. The

---

[1] Cf. also " The Lancastrian Constitution," by T. F. T. Plucknett, in *Tudor Studies*, edited by R. W. Seton-Watson.

contemporary with whom he is most naturally compared is
Pecock—who ventured even to assert that Aristotle had
sometimes been wrong, and in any case was nothing but an
" ensearcher to find out truth, as other men were, and are."
Yet in religion it is impossible to trace in Fortescue any
shade of influence either of Reformation or Renaissance.
He was entirely orthodox; in the *De Natura Legis Naturæ*
he expressly and in advance withdraws any statement that
may, unknown to him, savour of heresy, or be condemned
by the Church.

Fortescue's opinions on the papal power are curiously
opposed to his view of limited monarchy. The Pope is
Summus Pontifex, having supreme power, to whom all
earthly power is subject, even to the kissing of his feet
(*summam habens potestatem, cui omnis potestas terrena, usque
ad pedum oscula, est subiecta*). This he takes for granted
without discussion. Dr Figgis sums up the views of the
Conciliar writers as a belief that the most perfect possible
constitution, left by Christ to his Church, was a polity—
a mixed 'or limited monarchy—in which the monarch is
checked by a continual Council and both by a large representative body. This belief, though propped up by appeals
to Aristotle, was actually drawn from the facts of the political
world of their day. Now Fortescue was perfectly content
to hold one theory for the secular state and another for the
Papacy. He never argues from one to the other. He
recognises General Councils as an institution well established, to which the king must count upon sending his
representatives and procurators. Yet the Pope is both
Rex and *Sacerdos*, and " compelleth all princes as well
temporal as spiritual to come to his Great Councils."
Fortescue lived, perhaps, a generation too late to have been
touched by the Conciliar theory. Mr Plummer says : " It
is evident that Fortescue was strongly influenced by the

82

papal reaction which followed the Council of Constance."
Yet it is fair to notice that these papalist sentiments occur
in his recantation of Lancastrian views, in the midst of a
very strained argument and piece of special pleading.

Even in his personal religion Fortescue was little more
than an extremely cautious Job, looking out, a trifle puzzled,
at the spectacle of the wicked flourishing like a green bay-
tree. He wrote a little *Dialogue between Faith and Understanding*, in which his resigned yet troubled attitude stands
out very clearly and individually. " Alas, how many just
and peaceable creatures have borne the pain and anguish
of this war ! Alas, how many men of honest living have
suffered death ! . . . I see the naughty and reproveable
people helped with riches, and the good honest people
beggars and needy."

The only solution he can reach is to remind himself
again and again of the greatness of God. " Canst thou,
as thou supposest, know the just man from the sinner, and
be ascertained of the secret thoughts which God hath
reserved to Himself ? " " Art thou not remembered how it
is written that lack of justice and untrue deeds make realms
ready to be changed ? " Or again : " The Word of God
over-cometh our judgments and judgeth them, and His
infinite power justifieth all His works in doing them, for He
is a Justice of Himself." The Chief Justice is not to be led
away by any trouble or tragedy beyond his consistent conviction : " Shall not the Judge of all the earth do right ? "

What is specially noticeable about this little tract is not
the depth or courage of its thought ; it is remarkable for
neither, but for the fact that in the fifteenth century it bears
witness to the vivid personal religion of a busy man of
politics—a religion limited but undegraded by the degradation of the Church, untouched by the materialisation of
religious teaching. Fortescue's religion—the religion of a

83

layman—rings as true as the cloistered devotion of Thomas à Kempis. The only hint of modernity lies in the fact that he, a layman, writes of religion in English, and thereby links himself with the long movement of thought that produced the English Bible.

It remains only to attempt some brief general estimate of Fortescue's place in the political thought of England and of Europe.

Not only is he one of the earliest writers on comparative jurisprudence, and in some degree a forerunner of Machiavelli in his close intertwining of the theory of politics and the facts of history; not only was he a practical statesman and a revered judge; he was also one of the strongest influences both in suggesting the machinery of the Tudor despotism and in inspiring the Stuart lawyers in their revolt against that despotism. This apparent paradox is due to the fact that Fortescue never quite followed his argument as far as it would lead. He knew who should compose the Council; he never really faced the question who should choose them. He knew that Parliament was independent of the judges, but he never discussed the membership of Parliament nor the qualifications of electors. Hence his influence is felt by both parties, just as some of his opinions tend to face both ways. The Tudors worked on from his technical and practical experience; the lawyers of the seventeenth century inherited and employed his principle.[1]

But the more we study the principles behind Fortescue's life and work the more convinced we grow that he is not typical of the Renaissance—that he is just an Englishman, wise above the average, honest above the average;

---

[1] I do not propose to go farther into the question of Fortescue's influence on later generations, for it has been most admirably worked out by Dr Skeel in the *Transactions of the Royal Historical Society* for 1916. Little or nothing could be added to her treatment of the subject.

sane, scholarly, yet practical; a lover of books, who could throw away books when necessary, and rely upon experience; a lover of justice, tolerant, humane, patient, talking little of liberty, still less of freedom of thought, yet spending laborious days and nights in endeavouring to give to his fellows that justice which is the tangible side of liberty. He had been in France, and he thought little indeed of the character and habits of Frenchmen ; he had been in Scotland, and returned critical of the Scot ; he made no claim to be cosmopolitan in his sympathies : he is frankly insular, not from ignorance, but by preference.[1]

He was emphatically an Englishman living at the period to which the Renaissance is commonly assigned : if he belongs to the Renaissance it is to that peculiar native form of the movement which I tried to define in the early part of this lecture, and which to the average Englishman appears infinitely wiser and sounder than the ecstasies of the Italian or the furies of the German Renaissance.

After such an inconclusive conclusion, perhaps I may be thought merely arrogant if I borrow for my final sentence the very words of Fortescue : " Since the intention is answered wherewith you were moved to this conference, time and reason require that we put an end to it."

A. E. Levett

---

[1] His *Monarchia* has indeed been translated into German, but the editor found hardly an original reflection to make upon it.

BIBLIOGRAPHY

The Works of Sir John Fortescue, collected and arranged by Thomas (Fortescue), Lord Clermont. 2 vols. 1869.

FORTESCUE, SIR JOHN: *The Governance of England: otherwise called the Difference between an Absolute and a Limited Monarchy*. Edited with notes by Charles Plummer. 1885.

FORTESCUE, SIR JOHN: *Commendation of the Laws of England*. The translation into English of *De Laudibus Legum Angliæ*, by Francis Grigor. 1917 (reprint of edition of 1825).

SKEEL, C. A. J.: "The Influence of the Writings of Sir John Fortescue," in *Transactions of the Royal Historical Society*, 1916, 3rd series, vol. x.

English Historical Review. (*a*) 1911: note by J. P. Gilson on a literary fragment, possibly by Fortescue. (*b*) 1912: document and note by Miss Cora Scofield.

HOLDSWORTH, W. S.: *History of English Law*, vol. ii.

IV

NICOLO MACHIAVELLI

I

NO one who visits Hereford Cathedral can fail to be struck by the marvellous *Mappa Mundi* of Richard de Haldingham, which adorns the south choir aisle. It represents the theological conception of the world at the close of the thirteenth century. The habitable earth which it portrays is flat and circular, like a rimless plate, surrounded by a narrow fringe of ocean. At the centre of the circle stands Jerusalem; at the extreme east the Garden of Eden; midway between the two the Tower of Babel. Round the margin at different points are situated such places as the peninsula in which Gog and Magog were interned by Alexander the Great, the Earthly Paradise discovered by St Brandan, and the British Isles. On various otherwise unoccupied spots in Asia and Africa are to be found such interesting curiosities as the kingdom of Prester John, the realm of the Amazons, the granaries of Joseph, and the land of the Sciapodes, those fascinating one-legged folk whose solitary foot was so large and adaptable that it not only carried them about with incredible celerity, but also served them when they rested as a shelter from the tropical sun. It would be difficult to conceive any map which, in all its details, is more widely and wildly remote from correspondence with geographical reality. For even when it does present such features as the British Isles or the Mediterranean Sea which undoubtedly exist, it presents them in such forms and positions as make them almost unrecognisable. We may safely say that not even in the thirteenth century did it ever occur to any master mariner to borrow this map, or make a copy of it, for purposes of navigation. We may also confidently assert that if he had done so his voyage would have resulted in speedy and irretrievable disaster.

At the very time, however, when the pious prebendary of Haldingham was concocting from the Scriptures and the mythologies this fantastic travesty of the world as it actually exists, Italian seamen—particularly those of Venice and Genoa—on the basis of careful observation and repeated experiment, were constructing for practical purposes *portolani*, or mariners' charts, which give an amazingly accurate and minute representation of that Mediterranean basin wherein the main maritime commerce of the Middle Ages was concentrated. Free from prejudice and prepossession, unhampered by the postulates of theology, they depicted lands and seas as they really were, and so laid the foundations of the modern science of navigation.

All which is a parable and an analogy. Richard de Haldingham was a contemporary of St Thomas Aquinas and Dante. While he was drawing his fantastic map they were expounding the principles of politics. And the principles of politics as expounded by them bore, in respect of remoteness from reality, a striking resemblance to Richard's cosmology. They both lived ideally in a unified and symmetrical society—the *Respublica Christiana*—whose supreme ruler was God, and whose final law was His Holy Will. This society was administered mediately by two human agents, the Pope and the Emperor, the one exercising divine authority over all causes spiritual, the other over all causes temporal. Under the Pope served a hierarchy of cardinals, bishops, and clergy; under the Emperor a corresponding hierarchy of kings, nobles, and knights.

NICOLO MACHIAVELLI

The only serious problem that disturbed the beatific serenity of either St Thomas or Dante was the problem of the relation between the two powers, the spiritual and the temporal. Were they co-ordinate and equal, or was one superior to the other? How were the spheres of their jurisdiction delimited? As to these problems the views of St Thomas and Dante differed. To the one the Papacy from its very nature was the higher power; to the other the Empire had an immemorial claim to universal authority. The arguments by which these rival contentions were supported were drawn from precisely the same sources as those from which Richard de Haldingham filled his map with visionary shapes and imaginary names. They were arguments from the Scriptures, from the Fathers, from classical mythology, from supposed natural history. They turned upon the story of the Creation; upon the relation of the sun to the moon; of the soul to the body, of eternity to time; upon Samuel's attitude to Saul; upon the offerings of the Magi to the infant Lord; upon the sufficiency of the two swords possessed by Peter in the garden; upon the Saviour's parting command to the Apostles, and upon a multitude of other similar irrelevancies. They were, indeed, scholastic exercises almost wholly devoid of any relation to the actual politics of their age. For, at the very moment when Richard de Haldingham was moving with his map to Hereford, and while Dante was still in his prime, the Papal Monarchy, which St Thomas had exalted to the sky, passed from the humiliation of Anagni to the debasement of the " Babylonish Captivity " at Avignon. Similarly, the Holy Roman Empire, to which Dante looked for the unification and pacification of mankind, sank to the condition of a mere German overlordship, and even in that limited sphere ceased to function, since it failed to give even to Germany either unity or peace.

In short, while mediæval champions of Papacy and Empire were contending in the academic empyrean for the prize of a visionary world-dominion, actual authority over the men of a distracted and disrupted Christendom was being divided among a number of secular princes, out of whose mortal conflicts and diabolical intrigues the modern state-system was being evolved. Unchecked by either papal or Imperial authority, regardless of both canon and civil law, emancipated alike from the restraints of religion and of ethics, the " new monarchs " of the political jungle were displaying in a desperate struggle for existence those qualities of the lion and the fox which in the earlier ages of the cosmic process of biological evolution had enabled the animal possessors of these qualities to survive and prevail. The weapons in this fierce political struggle for existence were war and diplomacy. On the one hand, new armies, new means of offence and defence, new tactics and strategy, and, above all, a new ferocity, completely changed the military art from what it had been during the Middle Ages. On the other hand, missions, embassies, royal visits, supplemented by dispatches, memoranda, and reports, instituted a new science of diplomacy in which craft and guile found a limitless field for exercise. The princes who had to defend themselves in arms against a circle of powerful, alert, and merciless foes, and to protect themselves diplomatically against the conspiracies and intrigues of countless malignant rivals both within and without their states, had no use for the lofty speculations of Aquinas or Dante respecting the two powers, the two lights, the two swords, and the general duality of things. What they required was not a *Mappa Mundi* giving them sanctified information respecting the imaginary situation of the Garden of Eden, the Tower of Babel, and the kingdom of Prester John ; it was a *portolano* providing, in the form of a precise chart, the data indispensable for the navigation of the stormy and rock-infested seas on which their frail barques were tossing. It was such a *portolano* that Machiavelli professed to provide. His prime achievement, indeed, was to change the method of political speculation ; to make it once again, as it had been in Aristotle's day, inductive and historical ; to bring it back from the heavens to the earth ; to render it (so he hoped) practical and useful. He converted an abstract political philosophy, subordinate to ethics and theology, into an independent art of government divorced from both morals and religion.

II

Nicolo Machiavelli was born at Florence in 1469. This was the year in which Lorenzo the Magnificent began that period of uncrowned principality (1469–92) wherein the splendid city of Machiavelli's birth attained the summit of its glory and assumed the undisputed leadership in the scholarship, the thought, and the art of the Renaissance. It was also, by a coincidence, the year in which occurred the marriage of Ferdinand of Aragon and Isabella of Castile—an event which some historians speak of as marking the beginning of modern history, since it led to the unification of the Christian powers of the Peninsula, the conquest of Granada, the discovery of America, and the establishment of a century of Spanish ascendancy in Europe. It was significant that Machiavelli should thus have been born in the heyday of the Renaissance, and that he should have spent his youth amid the vast and rapid changes which inaugurated the era of the modern national states. For no one of whom we have record so early or so completely divested himself of the Middle Ages, or displayed himself so nakedly to his contemporaries, as the New Man.

Of his early life we know little. His family was Tuscan, old and noble. His father, Bernardo, followed the law, and occasionally held public appointments in Florence : he was also a landowner in a small way, drawing rents which were sufficient to relieve him—and his son Nicolo after him—from the fear of extreme poverty. Nicolo, although he soon showed an acuteness of mind which raised him above the level of his family and his neighbours, did not receive a very elaborate education : he learned to write Latin, but apparently not to read Greek. " The comparative restriction of his culture," says Villari, in words which should cheer and console modern undergraduates, " had the inestimable advantage of preserving the spontaneous originality of his genius and his style, and preventing them from being suffocated beneath a dead weight of erudition." So long as the rule of the Medici endured in Florence Machiavelli had, it would seem, no regular occupation. But the expulsion of Lorenzo's unworthy son, Piero, by the French in 1494, and the establishment of the republic, opened to him the way of civic employment. His study of Livy and Polybius had made him convincedly republican in sentiment. He looked with enthusiasm to the renewal in Florence of the great days of antique Rome, and he held the fervent hope that through the Florence of his day, as through the Rome of two thousand years earlier, Italy would attain to unity and peace.

At first, it would appear, Machiavelli attached himself to Savonarola, who, then in the flood-tide of his influence, was preaching the salvation of Italy through moral reform and religious revival, under French domination. But Machiavelli lacked moral sense, was entirely devoid of religious faith, and was filled with a loathing for foreigners. Hence he soon drew away from the agitating friar, and viewed with approval the means that were employed to extinguish him (1498). In both the *Discourses* and *The Prince* he examines with cold precision the cause of Savonarola's collapse : it was, he decided, that he was unarmed, and that behind the fury of his empty words, and the passing frenzy which he roused in the fickle populace, there was no *force* on which he could rely for the realisation of his ideals. Machiavelli came to the conclusion, which all his subsequent experience confirmed, that *force* directed by craft is the only thing that counts in politics.

This subsequent experience of his was varied and important. In 1498 he was appointed secretary to the so-called Second Chancery, otherwise known as " The Ten " —an administrative body specially concerned with the conduct of diplomacy and war. This office he held for fourteen years, that is, until 1512, when the republican constitution under which he served was overthrown and the Medicean tyranny restored. He performed his duties as a Secretary of State with conspicuous zeal, ability, fidelity, and success. In 1502, when his friend Piero Soderini—to whom he refers in many passages of his writings—was appointed perpetual Gonfalonier, he became, as his confidential adviser and trusted agent, one of the most influential men not only in Florence, but in Italy as a whole. His high position and the growing recognition of his exceptional powers of mind caused him to be sent by the Florentine Signory on a number of important military and political missions. On the one hand, he had to raise troops, hire mercenaries, make alliances, secure auxiliaries, and even conduct operations, in the long-drawn war with Pisa. On the other hand, he had to visit many Courts and camps, in order that he might counter conspiracies against his beloved city, break up hostile confederations, secure the withdrawal of unreasonable demands, and cement doubtful friendships.

His task was a far from enviable one. Since the death

of Lorenzo de' Medici in 1492 a new and critical condition of things had arisen in Italy. The foreigners had begun to pour their armies into the peninsula. The French invasion of 1494 had been followed by incursions of Spaniards, Germans, and Swiss, until Italy had become the battleground of the ferocious monarchs and marauders of the New Europe. It was the French with whom Florence, and Machiavelli as its representative, had most to do. The French had driven out the Medici in 1494; the French were the nominal allies of the Florentines in their efforts to conquer the intractable city of Pisa (which was supported by Spain and the Empire); the French were their main bulwark against the machinations of Cæsar Borgia and the exiled Piero de' Medici. The Florentine Republic, in short, existed only by sufferance of the French, and the French king, Louis XII, was entirely aware of the fact. Hence neither he nor his subordinates felt it at all necessary to conceal their contempt for Florence, their indifference to Machiavelli, or their complete unconcern as to what anyone in Tuscany said or did. They mulcted the Florentines of money; they subjected them to the grossest insults; they deserted them in critical emergencies; they finally left them naked to the vengeance of their foes. Four times was Machiavelli sent to Louis XII to plead for better treatment, and the humiliations which he was compelled impotently to suffer ate like a red-hot iron into his soul. How was it, he asked, that the French were so much stronger than the Italians that they could do with them what they liked? How was it that they could march from end to end of their peninsula without opposition; could sack their cities, overthrow their governments, plunder their treasures, slay their men, and violate their women, with complete impunity? How was it that the representative of an Italian state, such as Florence—a state eminent throughout

94

Christendom in commerce, finance, art, and learning—could be treated with a contempt reserved in other lands for serfs and dogs ? The answer, to Machiavelli, was plain : the Italians lacked political unity, and the small states among which they were divided lacked, whether singly or in combination, military power.

III

The two obvious weaknesses of Italy in Machiavelli's day were, indeed, political disunion and military incapacity.

The outstanding political phenomenon of the period was the formation of strong national states in the west of Europe. First, England had attained to unity and self-consciousness during the long and fiery process of the Hundred Years War. The subsequent Wars of the Roses, by eliminating the feudal nobility, had completed her consolidation. Under the firm and patriotic rule of the Tudor kings she had begun to enjoy peace, prosperity, power. Secondly, France had grown from a distracted collection of ungovernable fiefs into a mighty monarchy. One by one the great lordships had been subordinated to the Crown, until, with the acquisition of Burgundy and Brittany in Machiavelli's own time, the direct royal authority had been established over all the vast territory of the realm. Thirdly, Spain had arisen, as if by miracle, from the chaos and confusion of eight centuries of religious conflict and civil war. The Christian states of Leon, Castile, Navarre, Aragon, Catalonia, had all been brought under the rule of the joint monarchs Ferdinand and Isabella. The last Moorish enclave, Granada, had been absorbed. A vigorous religious unity had been impressed upon a newly created and proudly conscious Spanish nation.

Even in Germany a national spirit was moving—a spirit

95

which was destined, ere the end of Machiavelli's life, to manifest itself in the upheaval of the Reformation. The Emperor Maximilian, moreover, amid the distractions of his diversions and dissipations, was striving to re-establish some sort of central government, with courts and councils, military forces, and calculable revenue. Machiavelli anticipated the speedy unification of Germany, in spite of Maximilian's ineffectiveness, because it already had a titular head, because it possessed racial homogeneity, because it was peopled by men accustomed to war, but above all because it was the home in a special degree of such virtue as still remained upon the earth.[1]

The case of Italy, however, was very different. Intellectually and æsthetically in the van of all European peoples, morally and politically she lagged far in the rear. Her people, widely diverse in race and culture, were utterly degenerate and corrupt; she had lost all military capacity; her princes were craven and criminal; her Church was secularised and incredibly depraved; she was torn by violent schisms and incessant intrigues. No bond of any sort of unity held together her struggling atoms. The task of consolidating her, and making a nation of her, seemed to be beyond the reach of any normal means. And yet consolidated, nationalised, re-created, she must be, if she were to hold her own with the New Monarchs, if she were to be able to expel the foreign invaders, if she were to succeed in restoring order and in suppressing the orgy of villainy by which she was degraded and disgraced.

Five main states divided the peninsula between them. In the north the duchy of Milan and the republic of Venice contended for dominance in the Lombard Plain and for control of the eastern passes of the Alps. In the south the kingdom of Naples, under a line of illegitimate and treacherous

---

[1] Cf. *Discourses on Livy,* I, 55.

Aragonese rulers, contended for power and dominion against a resistant and fulminating Papacy. Between the two pairs of combatants Tuscany, under the hegemony of Florence, held a fluctuating balance. Normally, the Papacy and Venice were allied against Milan and Naples; but departures from the norm were frequent and bewildering. Hence the study of Italian politics in the fifteenth and sixteenth centuries is like an attempt to solve a complicated puzzle. One dominant fact, however, emerges from the study. It is that in the game of politics as played in Italy at that time no rules of honour or morality whatsoever were observed. Treasons, betrayals, poisonings, assassinations, perjuries, hypocrisies, sacrileges, infidelities— all kinds of base and hateful villainies—were employed without scruple or remorse. The Papacy in particular, under such Popes as Sixtus IV, Alexander VI, and Julius II, forgetting its sacred nature, and ignoring its international responsibilities, made itself notorious for its violence, selfishness, treachery, and mendacity. Machiavelli came to regard it as the root cause of Italy's disunion and debasement.

Another cause, however, the importance of which profoundly impressed him, was the military weakness of the Italians. Individual Italians, such as Castruccio Castracani of Lucca (whose life he made the basis of a notable romance), showed, it is true, both bravery and capacity. But the people of the peninsula, as a whole, were soft and effeminate, cowardly and unwarlike, engrossed in commerce and finance, distracted from virtue by philosophy and art, debilitated by sensuality, depraved by scepticism. They were, indeed, extremely quarrelsome, and they were experts in the use of poison and the dagger; but they preferred to wage their wars by proxy—that is, by means of companies of hired mercenaries, or by means of armies of auxiliaries drawn from foreign lands. So long as Italy's

97

quarrels were merely domestic this did not matter much. Her wars became little more than bloodless games, wherein treachery and bribery played a more decisive part than force or military skill. But it was another matter when she had to deal with the hosts of the new nations who came across the mountains or the seas to slay, to plunder, and to subjugate.

Northern Europe had been undergoing a military revolution. The days of feudal levies, armour-clad knights, battlemented castles, and picturesque chivalry were over. Everywhere national armies—large forces of foot-soldiers drawn mainly from the third estate—equipped with new weapons, and supported by that satanic novelty, artillery, were making havoc of old military conventions, transforming the art of war, and reconstructing the political framework of the Continent. First France, by the famous Ordonnance of Orleans in 1439, had established the force which had finally cleared both Normandy and Aquitaine of the English, and brought the exhausting Hundred Years War to a victorious end. Spain, Switzerland, the states of Germany, all had followed suit. Even England was reorganising her national militia, and was building the Royal Navy, which was destined to enable her from time to time to determine the balance of power in Europe. Only Italy remained inept, her coast unprotected, her passes unguarded, her rich cities a prey to any invader, her fruitful plains open to every spoiler. What, to Machiavelli, appeared the remedy for this deplorable condition of affairs?

IV

For the salvation of Italy from internal disorder and external oppression Machiavelli looked principally to the military regeneration of the people. The Nation in Arms was his ideal. "All able-bodied men between the ages of seventeen and forty should be drilled so as to be always ready to defend their country." [1] The treacherous and ineffective mercenaries should be dismissed. The dangerous and doubtful aid of alien auxiliaries should be refused. Machiavelli was speaking of what he knew. He himself, in the course of the protracted struggle between Florence and Pisa, had had agonising experience of both the violent perfidy of the Italian *condottieri* and the perfidious violence of the French men-at-arms whom Louis XII had sent to the nominal aid of the republic. The net result of their operations had been the humiliation of Florence, the failure of all her schemes, and the exhaustion of her treasury.

In all his great political works Machiavelli gives this supreme military problem a prominent place. To take the works in the order of their composition. (1) In *The Prince* he devotes a whole section (chapters xii–xiv)— about one-eighth of the entire book—to the question. First he exposes, with numerous examples, the evils of the *condottieri* system : " If Italy," he says, " had not trusted so many years to mercenary troops, she would not now be ruined." He blames " the ecclesiastical princes, strangers to the art of war," for introducing the vicious practice, the final consequence of which is that " Italy has been overrun by Charles, pillaged by Louis, forced by Ferdinand, and disgraced by the Switzers." Secondly, he treats of the perils which flow from the acceptance of the aid of foreign auxiliaries, and he illustrates his thesis by the disasters which accrued to Julius II from his Spanish allies, to Florence from its French levies, to the Byzantines from the Turkish stipendiaries, to Louis XI from the hired Swiss, and to the later Roman Emperors from their Gothic *fœderati*. Finally, he emphasises the prime importance of

[1] *The Art of War*, Book I.

military skill to princes, and of military training to their people : " Princes," he asserts, " ought to make the art of war their sole duty and occupation, for it is peculiarly the science of those who govern. War and the several sorts of discipline and institutions relative to it should be their only pursuits, the only profession they should follow, and the object they ought always to have in view." Moreover, they " must above all things, as the very foundation of the whole business, be furnished with soldiers of their own natives."

(2) In the *Discourses on Livy*, using the Romans as examples, he shows why " mercenary soldiers were unprofitable " and contends that " it is necessary in the maintaining of a state, whether it be a republic or a kingdom, to arm the native subjects, as we see all those have done who with their armies have made any great conquests." [1] But if the mercenaries are unprofitable, foreign auxiliaries are much worse : " Of all kinds of soldiers the auxiliaries are the most dangerous—therefore a prince or a republic should rather take any other course than seek to bring auxiliary soldiers into his country." [2] The decadence of the Roman Empire began, he considers, when the Imperial armies ceased to be native and were recruited from Parthians and Germans.[3]

(3) *The Art of War*, one of Machiavelli's most noteworthy and original works, is, as its title implies, wholly devoted to this cardinal theme. Its seven books are cast in the form of dialogues, in which the successful Italian commander, Fabrizio Calonna, expresses the views that may be regarded as Machiavelli's own. " The fundamental idea of *The Art of War*," says Villari, " is that the best militia can be formed by arming the people, and that at all periods the infantry constitutes the backbone of an

[1] *Discourses*, I, 44.   [2] *Ibid.*, II, 20.   [3] *Ibid.*, II, 30.

army." [1]   Or, in the words put into the mouth of Fabrizio,
"We are taught by history and experience, that all states
must be based upon national arms, and that by these alone
can they be securely defended."   Machiavelli regards the
Roman legion as the supreme model for imitation, but he
considers that improvements in matters of detail are suggested by examination of the military systems of the Swiss,
Germans, and Spanish foot-soldiers of his own day.   He
describes his resultant ideal for an Italian national army.
It is curious—and it suggests the limitations of the literary
man when he is dealing with practical affairs—that he
would not equip his national force with firearms, but would
revert to javelins, pikes, swords, and bows and arrows!
Even artillery—which in his own day had played a decisive
part in the battles of Ravenna, Novara, and Marignano—
he regards as of little account.   "Cannon are so difficult
of management that if you aim ever so little too high their
shots pass over the enemy's head, and if you lower them in
the least they fire into the ground.   They are altogether
useless in a general engagement." [2]   Into Machiavelli's
detailed discussions of the methods of training a militia,
the conduct of armies in the field, the principles of strategy
and tactics, the manner of quartering troops, and finally
the theories of fortification, it is unnecessary for us to enter.
Suffice it to say that *The Art of War*, as a whole, is a pioneer
treatise : it holds the same eminent place in military science
as *The Prince* does in political science.   Moreover, the purpose of the two works is the same : it is the emancipation and unification of Italy.   Just as Machiavelli concludes
The Prince with the declaration, "The first Italian who will
follow my councils shall, to his immortal honour, succeed
in the magnanimous enterprise of freeing his country,"

[1] Villari, *The Life and Times of Machiavelli*, ii, 292.
[2] *The Art of War*, Book III.

so does he end *The Art of War* with the words, " I declare
to you that whichsoever of the princes now holding states
in Italy shall first enter upon this road, he will be the first
to become lord of this country."

(4) In the *History of Florence*, written toward the close
of his life, Machiavelli once more reverts to this dominant
military matter.   Again and again he emphasises his conviction that the *condottieri* have been the cause of Italy's
undoing, and his belief that her redemption can come only
by means of a return to the patriotic ways of the antique
legionaries of Rome.

Machiavelli did not limit himself to words.   During
the republican period of his life, in his official capacity,
he was able to secure authority from the Florentine Signory
to organise and equip a militia.   For six years (1506–12)
he toiled unremittingly at the task, persevering amid the
most disheartening difficulties.   In 1512, when the French
—the chief allies of the republic—were driven from Italy
by the Spaniards, Germans, and Swiss; when the hostile
Pope, Julius II, supported the exiled Medici in their efforts
to return; when all extraneous aid failed them—in 1512
the militia was put to the test of war.   At the first puff
of gunpowder it turned tail and fled !   The product of
Machiavelli's six years of devoted labour vanished into thin
air.   Florence fell; the Medici resumed their tyranny;
Machiavelli, having suffered imprisonment and torture,
passed into banishment.   He realised that Italy needed
not only arms, but a man.

V

Machiavelli's banishment to his country estate at San
Casciano provided him with leisure and opportunity to
ponder his past career, to consider the lessons of his

experience, and to reinforce his conclusions by parallels drawn from Roman history. But for the ruin of his political prospects in 1512 we should have had none of his great literary works, and save for his official documents he would have passed almost inarticulate into oblivion. As it was, he relieved the boredom of his enforced retirement from affairs by diligent reading, hard thinking, and voluminous writing; seeking, moreover, by means of his pen, to win his way back into the service of the state which he loved with the purest devotion of his life.

He wrote primarily of the things which he himself had seen and known. True, he discoursed largely on Livy. Nevertheless, he was a student of current politics rather than of history. His method was that of observation more than of research. He was, indeed, devoid of the historic spirit, and, if he drew extensively upon history in his works, he did so uncritically and unscrupulously, being concerned merely to find examples to support conclusions already reached. Legend suited him quite as well as fact. The source of his science of politics was, in truth, his own diplomatic experience. As Secretary of the Ten he had gone, as we have remarked, during the fourteen years of his service, on many important missions to Italian and other Courts. Of these numerous missions the four of outstanding significance were those to Louis XII in 1500, to Cæsar Borgia in 1502, to Pope Julius II in 1506, and to the Emperor Maximilian in 1507. The first and the last of these four had taken him beyond the Alps; had revealed to him peoples vaster and more virile than the Italians; had opened his eyes to the meaning of nationality, patriotism, and civic virtue; had filled him with speculations as to the means by which the heterogeneous populations of his own country—cultivated but corrupt, intellectually renascent but morally decadent, individually quick but politically dead—could be welded together and vitalised with a spirit of unity. His speculations had taken rough shape in the dispatches which he had sent from time to time to the Ten, and so gradually in his official writings an art of government had begun to formulate itself. Thus a series of political *portolani* had come into existence, specially constructed to enable the statesmen of the Florentine republic to steer the frail barque of their defenceless city amid the storms of the tempestuous dawn of the modern era, and among the shifting quicksands of the peculiarly treacherous diplomacy of the time. A state which had no native army, but was at the mercy of hired *condottieri* and alien auxiliaries, had to depend for the continuance of its precarious existence upon the craft and subtlety of its politicians. Machiavelli had sought in his masterly dispatches to guide the helpless and distracted Signory along ways of security.

His mission to the camp of the warlike Pope Julius II had been important in that it had confirmed him in his opinion that the prime cause of Italy's disruption was the existence of the States of the Church, and that the most formidable obstacle to the unification of the peninsula was the temporal power of the Papacy. This conviction remained with him to the end of his days. His last work, his unfinished *History of Florence*, although it was written by order of a cardinal and was dedicated to a Pope, is inspired throughout by a fierce and freely avowed detestation of clerical rule. Having in the introductory book portrayed the sad condition of Italy, Machiavelli concludes —to quote Villari's summary—" The sole remedy for these evils is the institution of a national army under the rule of a prince able to organise and command his troops, and to use them for the defence and unity of the country, by abasing the power of the Papacy, emancipating and

104

fortifying the State, and leaving at his death a legacy of good laws and civil institutions towards the establishment of liberty."[1]

The abasement of the power of the Papacy, however, requires, he perceives, the effective existence of a national army; and the effective existence of a national army necessitates the rule of an autocratic and capable prince. What sort of a person must the prince be who, in the desperate circumstances of the time, can carry through this titanic project of unification? The answer to this question had been provided by the experience which Machiavelli had gained on the most remarkable of all his diplomatic missions, namely, that to the moving camp of Cæsar Borgia in 1502—at Urbino, Imola, Cesena, Sinigaglia.

In 1502 Cæsar Borgia, son of Pope Alexander VI, had been engaged in his father's name, but on his own behalf, in reducing the Romagna. Nominally a portion of the States of the Church, the Romagna had, during the eclipse of the Papacy in the Captivity and the Schism, passed into the hands of a number of petty tyrants, whom it had proved impossible to dispossess or control. Cæsar, having procured from the papal Curia the cession of the Romagna as a dukedom, had been employed in expelling the tyrants and establishing an orderly government. Having few forces of his own, he had been compelled to operate with mercenaries under such leaders, then noted, as Paolo Orsini, Vitellozzo Vitelli, and Oliverotto of Fermo. But he had been mainly dependent on Gascon and Swiss auxiliaries provided under treaty by Louis XII of France. His little war had raged within a few miles of the Tuscan frontier, and Florence had been perturbed both by raids into her territories and also by pressing demands on Cæsar's part for men

[1] Villari, *The Life and Times of Machiavelli*, ii, 394.

and money. Machiavelli had been sent—at first nominally under Bishop Francesco Soderini—to Cæsar's headquarters to ward off the Duke's hostility, mitigate his demands, and if possible safeguard Florence from injury and spoliation. On the whole, he had succeeded in his purpose, and he had secured the cordial commendation of the Signory. The fifty-two letters, still extant, which he had penned from the Borgian base contain not only the most vivid and authentic of all existing pictures of Duke Cæsar at the height of his fortune, but also a clear forecast of that science of statecraft which ten years later Machiavelli was to embody in *The Prince*.

For some six months in 1502 Machiavelli had had the formidable Cæsar under close and almost constant observation. Although his diplomatic enemy, engaged with him in an incessant contest of subtlety and wit, yet he had acquired for him an immense admiration. His quickness, his courage, his secrecy, his terrific vigour, his iron resolution, his remorseless severity, his amazing success, had filled Machiavelli with wonder and envy. He had contrasted his mode of procedure with the slow, vacillating, inept feebleness of the Florentine Signory. In particular, he had watched with the most profound interest and appreciation the way in which he had succeeded in emancipating himself from his faithless mercenaries, and in rendering himself independent of his dangerous French auxiliaries, by winning the confidence of his new subjects and building up a native army. In Cæsar Borgia Machiavelli had found a prince who might, if fortune had continued to favour him, have accomplished the desire of his heart. In Cæsar Borgia's methods he had seen what appeared to him to be the only means by which the revivification of Italy could be effected, the foreigner expelled, and unity achieved.

VI

Machiavelli's sympathies were wholly republican ; one of the finer traits in his cynical and repellent character is his faith in the people—a faith, we may remark, not very easy to reconcile with his pessimistic estimate of individual human nature. If ever the clarity of his style begins to glow with the warmth of generous emotion it is when he speaks of the virtues of the Roman commonwealth or the liberties of his native city. His *Discourses on Livy* are eloquent of democratic enthusiasm, and it was the reading of them to the select assembly which used to meet in the Oricellarii Gardens which inspired the Soderini conspiracy against the Medicean tyranny in 1522.[1] But he was entirely aware that republican institutions are possible only to a virtuous people ; that is to say, to a people courageous, simple and pure in life, self-sacrificing, devoted to the service of the State and zealous for the common weal. Such a people were the ancient Romans of whom he read credulously in the First Decade of Livy and in the voluminous eulogies of Polybius. Such too, he thought, were the Swiss and the Germans of his own day. But such were *not* the contemporary Italians. His experiences in Florence, especially in relation to his militia, coupled with his observations in the Papal States, Venice, Milan, and Naples, all filled him with the conviction that, although Italy might be ready for republicanism when she should have been disciplined, united, regenerated, yet in her existing condition her only hope lay in the stern and strong autocracy of a militant and politic prince—such a prince as Cæsar Borgia had been in his prime, such a prince as Giuliano or Lorenzo de' Medici might conceivably be.

By what means should a prince seek to attain to ascend-

---

[1] Villari, *The Life and Times of Machiavelli*, ii, 333.

ancy in such an Italy as that of Machiavelli's day, and, having attained to it, by what means should he seek to keep it ? That is the question which Machiavelli set himself to answer in the most famous—or infamous—of all his works, the treatise entitled *Il Principe*. This brief but pungent treatise, written in the latter half of the year 1513, was composed for, dedicated to, and intended for the exclusive perusal of the Medicean tyrant who had overthrown the Florentine republic the year before. It is imperative that those who read it should realise that they were not meant to do so. It was not written for them. It was a paper of private and confidential instructions prepared for the personal and peculiar use of a particular individual. It was not a general dissertation on the science of politics or the art of government. It was not compiled for publication, nor was it in fact published until five years after Machiavelli's death (1532), when an injudicious Pope—Clement VII, cousin of the man to whom it had been dedicated—imprudently let it loose upon the world. Its whole efficacy depended upon its *not* being published: for in vain is the snare set in the sight of any bird! The very success of such craft and guile as Machiavelli commends hangs upon the faith in the honesty and sincerity of the deceiver. To proclaim to the world that you are going to tell lies renders it useless for you to do so. Your very truth is not believed.

The Prince, then, is a *vade mecum* dedicated to the use of the Medici—first Giuliano; secondly, after Giuliano's death in 1516, Lorenzo. That Machiavelli should have sought to serve the Medici is, indeed, at first sight, surprising ; for the whole of his public life had been spent in trying to prevent their return to Florence ; and when, in spite of him, they had come back he had suffered much inconvenience at their hands—including dismissal from office, exile, imprisonment, and torture on the rack.   When, in fact, *The Prince* passed into circulation it was its dedication to the Medici rather than its surrender to the devil that caused astonishment and adverse criticism in Italy. It was not its obvious abandonment of morality, but its apparent desertion of the republican cause which excited scandal and demanded explanation.   To us the explanation is fairly clear : Italy, in Machiavelli's opinion, needed a despot ; and Machiavelli quite obviously needed and desired employment.   Hence he addressed the Medici, who at the moment were doubly powerful in the possession of both Tuscany and the Papacy.   On the one hand : " May your illustrious house, strong in all the hopes which justice gives our cause, deign to undertake this noble enterprise," *i.e.*, the deliverance and consolidation of Italy.[1] On the other hand : " If from your elevated position you should condescend to look down on a person in my lowly station, you will see how long and how unworthily I have been persecuted by the extreme and unrelenting malevolence of fortune." [2]

Apart from the Dedication, the twenty-six chapters of *The Prince* fall into five groups.   The first group (i–xi) treats of generalities, the greater part being devoted to the classification of principalities in respect of their nature and mode of acquisition.   In this section by far the most noteworthy chapter is that (vii) which contains Machiavelli's account of the meteoric career of Cæsar Borgia, whom he idealises, under the name of Valentino, until he becomes a mythological being, the embodiment of sheer, unmitigated statecraft.   He holds him up as a perfect model for a new prince who would secure himself in his principality. He does this with his eyes open, knowing intimately well the appalling crimes—murders, assassinations, treacheries,

---

[1] *The Prince*, ch. xxvii.   [2] *Ibid.*, Dedication.

duplicities, debaucheries, sacrileges—of which this terrible adventurer had been guilty. In one of his earlier writings, the so-called first *Decennale* (1504), he had truly and frankly described him as " a man without compassion, rebellious to Christ, the Hydra, the basilisk, deserving of the most wretched end." But in spite of this he exalts him in *The Prince* as a model, because he sees in his methods, frightful and immoral as they are, the only hope of success in the task which the New Prince has to face in the Italy of his day. What these methods are he reserves for explicit treatment in the third section of his work.

The second group of chapters (xii–xiv) is, as we have already remarked, devoted to military matters. Machiavelli writes with an obvious intensity of conviction. His purpose in writing is eminently practical: " My aim," he says, " is to write for the advantage of him who understands me." He descants on the curse of mercenary armies, his argument being pointed by the stories of how Sforza betrayed Naples, Vitelli Florence, and Carmagnola Venice. He passes on to treat of the peril of trusting to foreign auxiliaries, with instances drawn from the disasters which Italy has suffered at the hands of French and Spanish allies. Finally, he emphasises the importance of military skill to princes, and shows how they can acquire it—practically, by exercises and by the pursuit of the chase; theoretically, by the study of history and the lives of great commanders.

The third group of chapters (xv–xviii) brings us to the heart of the treatise, and displays to us the essence of what is called Machiavellism; that is to say, politics divorced from ethics. The keynote is struck in the sentence : " That man who will profess honesty in all his actions must needs go to ruin among so many that are dishonest; therefore it is necessary for a prince who desires to preserve himself to be able to make use of that honesty and to lay it aside as need shall require." And as with honesty, so with mercy and compassion. Then follows a detailed examination of the circumstances in which—quite irrespective of moral considerations—a prince should be liberal or parsimonious, cruel or merciful, faithful to his word or perfidious. The illustrations by means of which Machiavelli points his narrative throw a lurid light into the abysses of Italian politics in the Renaissance period, especially when, as his supreme example of successful mendacity and merciless treachery, Machiavelli selects Pope Alexander VI. To the problems raised by Machiavellism we must return in a moment. They are living and burning problems, and it is by reason of their continuing urgency that the present-day study of Machiavelli is worth while.

The fourth group of chapters (xix–xxv) sinks from the giddy heights of political non-morality attained in the preceding group down to a rather dull level of commonplace maxims of prudence. The prince is instructed how to avoid contempt and hatred, how to secure popularity, how to acquire respect and reputation, how to steer a happy mean between excessive *hauteur* and undue familiarity, and so on. The unhappy examples of Ferrante of Naples and Ludovico of Milan point the moral and adorn the tale.

The fifth and final division of *The Prince* consists of the solitary and magnificent twenty-sixth chapter, in which the Medici are exhorted to rise to the height of the great opportunity which lies before them, to establish their authority, to call the Italians to arms, to expel the barbarians, and to reign as saviours of their country. How does this splendid and stirring appeal—the herald cry of Italian national unity—accord with the diabolical devices described in chapters xv–xviii as appropriate for the realisation of the ideal ? Neither to Machiavelli nor to his contemporaries did there appear anything incongruous between a noble political end and grossly immoral means. How does the case seem to us ?

VII

Machiavelli was above and beyond all else a prophet and a preacher of the principle of patriotism and the idea of the national state. Now, on the one hand, the principle of patriotism seems to be a lower ideal than the cosmopolitan conception which had dominated the Middle Ages ; and the idea of the national state appears to be a less lofty one than the mediæval idea of a Universal Christendom based upon religion and ruled by a Vicegerent of God. But, on the other hand, it must be borne in mind that the mediæval principle of Christian brotherhood, and the mediæval ideal of an ecumenical Church-State, had never been even approximately realised in fact. The horrid actuality of the thousand years which separated Machiavelli from the deposition of Romulus Augustulus had been a weltering chaos of conflicting clans, struggling tribes, anarchic fiefs, and encroaching kingships, stirred up incessantly by rebellious bishops, and kept at the boil by fulminating Popes. Never had there been a more marked contrast between theory and practice; never had the *Mappa Mundi* been more entirely unrelated to the facts of human geography. Hence, if in the realm of abstract doctrine the national state suggested a decline from the unity of Christendom, in the realm of concrete politics it stood for an immense and incalculably beneficial advance upon the parochialism, localism, tribalism, and feudalism which had been the actual condition of the Dark Ages. Machiavelli clearly perceived the enormous advantages which France had gained by the absorption of the great fiefs, and by the centralisation of the government of the country under the Capetian and Valois kings. Not less clearly did he see the benefits which had accrued to Spain through her unification under the Catholic kings. From his observations he concluded that it was vitally necessary for Italy to pass through the same process of consolidation, and to attain to the same condition of unity.

The ideal form of national state which Machiavelli projected for Italy was undoubtedly a republic modelled upon the Roman commonwealth as portrayed by Livy. But he realised that the conditions which had rendered possible the unification of the peninsula under the old city-state were absent in his own day. If the consolidation of France and Spain had been effected only by means of the force and craft of exceptionally able monarchs, how much more did the disorder of Italy demand the exercise of the vigour, the subtlety, the swiftness, and the secrecy which an autocratic prince alone could provide! The all-important thing was the establishment of the national state. Both the form which it should take and the means by which it should be established were secondary concerns.

This question of means brings us to the heart of the Machiavelli problem. For the essence of Machiavellism is the doctrine that the end justifies the means. It implies the deliberate dissociation of politics from ethics, and the assertion that the plea of ' reasons of state ' is a sufficient answer to any and every accusation of cruelty or deceit. Perhaps the two clearest summaries of the doctrine presented by Machiavelli himself are the following, the first from the *Discourses*, the second from *The Prince* : " Where the deliberation is wholly touching the safety of the fatherland there ought to be no consideration of just or unjust, pitiful or cruel, honourable or dishonourable, but rather, all other respect being laid aside, that course ought to be taken which

may preserve the life and maintain the liberty thereof " ;[1]
and, " Let a prince, therefore, take the surest courses he
can to maintain his life and state ; the means shall always
be thought honourable "[2]—the means specially alluded
to by Machiavelli being those which he has just been
describing as analogous to the merciless ferocity of the lion
and the unscrupulous craftiness of the fox.   The statesman,
in Machiavelli's view, is emancipated from the ordinary
restraints of morality.   In the interests of his country he is
entitled, nay, is on occasion required, to commit acts of
violence and to perpetrate frauds which if performed on his
own account in private life would brand him as a criminal
and a scoundrel.   He must not shrink, if reasons of state
demand it, from any cruelty however great, or from any
perfidy however base.

That is Machiavellism.   It is the doctrine that terrorism and treachery are legitimate instruments in politics.
Machiavelli does not urge their indiscriminate use.   He
recognises the fact that they are dangerous instruments,
prefers the normal employment of the safer implements of
ethics, blames such operators as Agathocles of Syracuse
and Oliverotto of Fermo for employing them too freely.[3]
But, all the same, he regards them as essential elements
in the statesman's equipment, and he severely condemns
those who have failed to employ them when emergency
has demanded their use.   Romulus, he considers, was
justified in slaying his brother Remus, for unity of control
was necessary for the successful founding of Rome; hence
" though the act accuse him, the effect excuses him—for
though he that uses violence to waste is blameworthy, not
he that uses it for redress and order."[4]   Similarly he defends the sanguinary severity of Brutus after his overthrow

[1] *Discourses*, III, xli. [2] *The Prince*, ch. xxviii.
[3] *Ibid.*, ch. viii. [4] *Discourses*, I, ix.

of the Tarquinian monarchy, in words which might have
been employed by Lenin in 1917: " This is always well
known to those who read ancient stories, how that after
the change of a state, either from a republic into a tyranny
or from a tyranny into a republic, some memorable execution upon the enemies of the present condition is needful." [1]
Conversely he contemptuously condemns Gian Paolo
Baglioni of Perugia, who, when he was resisting the papal
claims to overlordship over his city, failed through squeam-
ishness and " base cowardice " to avail himself of a golden
opportunity of decisive victory and everlasting renown
which Fortune offered to him. Pope Julius II having
rashly visited Perugia, unguarded, together with twenty-
four cardinals, Gian Paolo omitted to exterminate the lot
of them. " He had not the courage," says Machiavelli,
" to do an exploit that every one would have admired, a
deed that would have given him an everlasting memory,
an act whose greatness would have surpassed all infamy." [2]
His weakness was aggravated by the fact that the cardinals
" had the best of all their jewels with them ! " Hence,
when some time afterward Pope Julius overthrew him and
strung him up on a gibbet, he paid a fitting penalty for his
indecision and lack of enterprise.

As with violence, so with craft and fraud : " How com-
mendable it is in a prince to keep his word and live with
integrity, not making use of cunning and subtlety, every
one knows well; yet we see by experience in these our days
that those princes have effected great matters who have
made small reckoning of keeping their words and have
known by their craft to turn and wind men about and in
the end have overcome those who have grounded upon
the truth." [3] And again, " It is necessary for a prince
that will achieve great matters to learn to be a cunning

[1] *Discourses*, III, iii.   [2] *Ibid.*, I, xxvii.   [3] *The Prince*, ch. xviii.

deceiver," [1] for "that man who will profess honesty in all his actions must needs go to ruin amongst so many that are dishonest. Wherefore it is necessary for a prince who desires to preserve himself to be able to make use of honesty or to lay it aside as need shall require." [2] Machiavelli in both *The Prince* and the *Discourses* gives many examples, drawn from history and his own observation, of what he regards as successful chicanery. But he reserves his highest eulogies for Pope Alexander VI, who, he says, " never did anything else than deceive men, and never meant otherwise, and always found whom to work upon." " Yet," he adds, " never was there a man who would protest more effectually, or aver anything with more solemn oaths and observe less than he; nevertheless, his deceptions all succeeded, for he knew how to play his part cunningly." [3]

If, however, Machiavelli admires one ruler for his consummate mendacity and another for his remorseless ferocity, he sees the perfect combination of the qualities of the lion and the fox—terrorism and treachery—in Cæsar Borgia, to whose baleful career he again and again recurs, as though irresistibly fascinated. Cæsar Borgia in 1502—the year of his highest power and luckiest fortune—supplies the perfect model of the methods by which alone, Machiavelli thinks, the overthrow of the *condottieri*, the expulsion of the foreigners, and the salvation of Italy can be secured.

VIII

What is the verdict of history upon Machiavellism—that is to say, upon the doctrine that the end justifies the means, that ethics have no relevance to politics, that reasons of state excuse all deviations from the moral law, and that Satan may properly be called in to cast out Satan? The

---

[1] *Discourses*, II, xiii.　　[2] *The Prince*, ch. xx.　　[3] *Ibid.*, ch. xviii.

verdict of history is, it seems to me, one of decisive condemnation and emphatic rejection. And yet the doctrine
has persisted, and still persists, with a strange vitality. In
the sixteenth century, in spite of the denunciation of both
Catholic and Protestant theologians, *The Prince* became the
text-book of monarchs ; while the unscrupulous practices
which it recognised established themselves as the common
devices of politicians. The massacre of St Bartholomew's
Day 1572, for instance, was regarded as a perfect exposition
of Machiavellian craft and violence. In the seventeenth
and eighteenth centuries, when the furies of the wars of
religion had died down, the more sanguinary aspects of
Machiavellism ceased to display themselves so conspicu-
ously as before, and its prime manifestations had to be
sought in the dark intricacies of diplomacy. Napoleon I,
however, was a Machiavellian in both senses of the term:
he believed equally in violence and in fraud as legitimate,
and at times necessary, instruments of policy. His sinister
influence dominated many of the makers of nineteenth-
century history, and his Machiavellian principles found
disciples and exemplars in such men as Metternich, Louis
Philippe, Napoleon III, Bismarck, and Cavour.

In the Italy of Cavour, indeed, a formal revival of the
Machiavellian cult took place in the middle of the nineteenth
century. Machiavelli was recognised and exalted as a
pioneer of the unification of the peninsula, and the methods
which he had suggested as necessary for the realisation of
his ideal in the sixteenth century were accepted as appropriate and inevitable in the later age. But it was in Germany
that the most formidable recrudescence of Machiavellism
took place. The philosophy of Hegel prepared the Teutonic mind for an exaltation of the State. The disintegration of the Fatherland after the Napoleonic wars made its
reconstruction on a national basis imperative. The task

of reconstruction was one of almost superhuman difficulty, and it seemed to call for methods of " blood and iron," and methods of craft and guile, similar to those which Machiavelli had expounded and Cæsar Borgia had exemplified. Hence men like Bismarck adopted and applied them, and men like Treitschke defended and glorified them. The apparent success of Machiavellian methods in the making of the German Empire caused the principles of *The Prince* to establish themselves as fundamental postulates of Prussian politics. In 1914 they received their perfect exposition in the shameless perfidy which violated the solemn guarantees of Belgian neutrality, and in the diabolical cruelty which sought to extinguish Belgian independence in agony and blood. From Germany, as part of the heritage of Karl Marx, Machiavellism spread to Russia, where since 1917 it has displayed itself in the appalling terrorism and abysmal treachery of Bolshevism. Hence we see now, even more clearly than Lord Morley could see when in 1897 he delivered his Romanes Lecture, that Machiavelli " represents certain living forces in our actual world," and that, as Lord Acton remarked, " he is a contemporary influence."

Nevertheless, I hold that both the conscience of mankind and the verdict of history have declared themselves decisively against Machiavellism. The one says that it is theoretically indefensible, the other that it is practically unsound. (1) *It is theoretically indefensible.* The State is not, as Machiavelli and his disciples regard it, an end in itself. It is merely a means to the good life of its members individually and collectively. It is a moral institution whose supreme purpose is the definition and maintenance of justice. *Justitia remota, quid aliud est regnum quam grande latrocinium :* in the absence of justice what is the state but organised brigandage on a large scale ? A state established for any other end than the realisation of the moral

NICOLO MACHIAVELLI

law had better not exist at all. And this ethical end cannot
be dissociated from the means by which its attainment is
sought. There must be congruity between the two. As
well might you expect to gather figs from thistles as look
for the fruit of justice from a root of violence and deceit.
(2) *It is practically a failure.* The verdict of history is that
Machiavellism has not in fact succeeded. In the long run
the lion and the fox dc .... p...ail; the cruelty of the one
and the craft of the other not only do not save them, but
are the very causes of their destruction. As Talleyrand
might have said, Machiavellism is worse than a crime ; it
is a mistake. In the sixteenth century Gentillet condemned
it because of the ruin which it brought to those who
practised it; in the seventeenth century Richelieu, who
had no moral objection to it, warned his king against it
because of its fatal consequences.[1] In the eighteenth
century Voltaire, who will not be suspected of Puritanism,
in a famous letter to Frederick the Great of Prussia—one
of the most consummate practitioners of the Machiavellian
politic—condemned the art of *The Prince*: " Cet art," he
said, " que l'on doit mettre à côté de celui des Locustes et
des Brinvilliers, a pu donner à quelques tyrans une puissance
passagère, comme le poison peut procurer un héritage ;
mais il n'a jamais fait ni de grands hommes ni des hommes
heureux, cela est bien certain." In the nineteenth century
Lord Morley concluded his Romanes Lecture in the same
strain. After expounding and denouncing the Machiavellian principle he says, " The effect was fatal even for his
own purpose, for what he put aside, whether for the sake
of argument, or because he thought them in substance
irrelevant, were nothing less than the living forces by which
societies subsist and governments are strong."
These weighty opinions are borne out by the chronicle

[1] Richelieu, *Testament Politique*, ii, 6.

of events. Machiavelli made shipwreck of his own life because with excessive subtlety and with shameless lack of principle he sought to run with the republican hare and hunt with the Medicean hounds; when in 1527 the Medici fell and the republic was restored he found that he had succeeded in earning the ineradicable distrust of both parties. Hence he was left to die in dishonour, disillusionment, destitution, ⸏⸏⸏ ⸏⸏⸏⸏. Similarly his hero, Cæsar Borgia, excited so unutterable a loathing and dread by his ferocity and perfidy that, wholly apart from ill-fortune, he was hounded out of Italy and sent to perish in the Pyrenees. The record of the Machiavellians in all ages is the same—a brief and unsubstantial triumph due to terror and surprise, followed by permanent and irretrievable ruin when the conscience and the courage of mankind have revived. In our own day the perfidy and barbarity of the Germans toward the Belgians, which they hoped would carry them to speedy victory in the autumn of 1914, were the very causes which brought Britain, Italy, and America into the War against them, and ensured their ultimate defeat. The similar and even more atrocious crimes of the Russian Bolsheviks—ruthless cruelty and bottomless mendacity erected into a system and avowed with a brazen effrontery never before equalled—have not as yet completely worked out their appropriate and inevitable catastrophe. But they are very near doing so. No self-respecting Power will touch their blood-stained hands; no Power of any sort can trust their perjured word. They are outcasts from the community of nations, and their only hope of a brief postponement of their doom is to extend to other countries the depredations with which they have desolated their own.

Signor Mussolini in Italy avows himself a Machiavellian and says, " I believe Machiavelli's *Prince* to be the statesman's supreme guide." If he means, as he appears to,

NICOLO MACHIAVELLI

no more than that a statesman must show strength, decision, resolution, all may be well. But if, as some of his followers seem to assume, he means that such deeds as the murder of Signor Matteotti are legitimate means of political procedure, then—as the conscience of Italy and the civilised world has made abundantly clear—his day of authority will be short.

To sum up the matter in a nutshell: Machiavelli with all his acuteness of observation had a singular faculty for failing to see factors of the first importance. Loudly as he professed to see things as they really were, he saw them as they really were not. Just as he depicted an art of war in which artillery played no part, so he depicted an art of government in which neither morals nor religion had any place. His estimate of human nature, on which his whole political system was based, was radically mistaken. He regarded man as entirely bad, and founded his system on that false assumption. He ignored goodness in man just as he ignored gunpowder in war. Goodness and gunpowder! Could a man of the early sixteenth century who professed to be practical have made two more colossal errors of omission? In the art of war the development of firearms has swept the Machiavellian precepts into ridicule and oblivion. In the art of politics the conscience of mankind has repudiated the Machiavellian maxims, and the experience of the human race has demonstrated their folly. The records of history tend to show that Socrates and Plato were right when they said that in the long run the knave and the fool are one and the same. For human society is established on moral foundations, and righteousness must in the end prevail.

THE EDITOR

BIBLIOGRAPHY

A. Primary Sources

Tutte le Opere di Nicolo Machiavelli. 1550.
Il Principe, edited by L. A. Burd, with an Introduction by Lord Acton. 1891.
The Prince, translated by N. H. Thomson. 1882.
Discourses on Livy, translated by N. H. Thomson. 1883.
Historical, Political and Diplomatic Writings of Machiavelli, translated by C. E. Detmold. 4 vols. 1882.

B. Secondary Sources

Burd, L. A.: " Machiavelli," in *The Cambridge Modern History*, vol. i. 1902.
Dunning, W. A.: *History of Political Theories, Ancient and Mediæval.* 1910.
Dyer, L.: *Machiavelli and the Modern State.* 1904.
Feuerlein, E.: "Zur Machiavelli-Frage," in *Historische Zeitschrift.* 1868.
Franck, A.: *Réformateurs et publicistes de l'Europe*, vol. i. 1864.
Macaulay, Lord: " Machiavelli," in *Critical and Historical Essays.* 1827.
Mancini, P. S.: *Prelezioni con un Saggio sul Machiavelli.* 1876.
Morley, Lord: *Machiavelli* (The Romanes Lecture, 1897).
Mundt, T.: *Nicolo Machiavelli und das System der modernen Politik.* 1867.
Nitti, F.: *Machiavelli nella Vita e nelle Opere.* 1876.
Owen, J.: *Skeptics of the Italian Renaissance.* 1893.
Symonds, J. A.: *The Renaissance in Italy*, vol. i, Chapters V and VI. 1875.
Tomasino, O.: *La Vita e gli Scritti di Nicolo Machiavelli.* 1883.
Villari, P.: *The Life and Times of Machiavelli* (translated by Linda Villari). 1878.

V

SIR THOMAS MORE

IT is perhaps true to say of More that we know him more familiarly than any other man of his century. Written in the first instance by his devoted admirers, his life has for us an intimacy that is indeed a valued possession. In this, strangely enough, he shares the good fortune of a man for whom he had but a qualified admiration. Cavendish's *Life of Wolsey* and Roper's *Life of More* stand in a place apart in early biography. Yet Wolsey's life has been subjected to a fiercer light than More's, and there are some who feel that More's life has yet to be written. Probably nothing worth the saying remains to be said about his *Utopia*, but much that ought not to have been said about the so-called intolerance of its author's later days has found a hearing mainly because we have not known our man.

That More attached very definite importance to the influence of the experience he gained in the household of John Morton, Archbishop of Canterbury, is indicated by his references to the old Cardinal not only in his *Utopia* but also in his *History of Richard III*.[1] His admiration for Morton is significant when we recall the insistence with which, as archbishop, he had pursued his determination to bring under his discipline his provincial monasteries, and particularly the powerful Benedictine house of St Albans. There was a rough, homespun virtue in Morton, a blunt directness that More admired, an intrepidity that

---

[1] For the question of More's authorship of *Richard III* see Joseph Delcourt, *Essai sur la langue de Sir Thomas More*, pp. 388 ff.

was not without influence on his admirer and struck in him an answering note. Morton was one of the great figures of the Renaissance in England, a good Englishman, a bold statesman, a wise builder, and a resolute reformer with a keen eye for soundness in essentials. While much of the first part of More's *Utopia* is taken up with his analysis of the evils of the day, social and economic, we are conscious that Morton stands out before us as a man to whom the reform of such things was a matter of moment. One remark of More's throws a strong light on the old man : " He took delight many times with rough speech to prove what prompt wit and bold spirit were in every man." And it was for the like qualities that Morton himself commended More, " in whose wit and towardness," Roper tells us, " the Cardinal much delighted."

In this household of Renaissance culture, enrolled as a chaplain, although he apparently never proceeded beyond the degree of acolyte (1490), when More was twelve years old was the dramatist Henry Medwall. I never lose an opportunity of introducing Medwall to the notice of those admirers of More who do not already know his play of *Fulgens and Lucres*. It is based on a translation of a pretty story written more than fifty years earlier by a Petrarchan humanist of Pistoja. In it we find for the first time in our drama a romantic comedy of purely secular and social interest. It has, moreover, an admirably comic underplot provided by two boys who step in among the players as Roper says More used to do. The only copy of the play that has survived was printed by More's brother-in-law, John Rastell, and although this copy has now gone to Mr Henry Huntington's library in California he has made it available for scholars in an edition in facsimile.

" For his better furtherance in learning " Morton placed More at Oxford (1492–4), where he came under the influence of Grocyn and Linacre. In after years, when, having resigned his Chancellorship, he called his family about him to discuss with them how they might best economise and what retrenchments they must make, he suggested as a fair level for their first descent a Lincoln's Inn diet. If need be they might sink to the fare of an Inn of Chancery, and, at the very worst, fall to Oxford fare, " so they kept companie and were merrie together." The passage from Morton's household to Oxford took all these stages in one leap, and his father, as if to bend him to his task and wean him of any softness developed in Morton's household, " so used the matter to the end that he should only follow his learning and study that he allowed him but only necessaries; nor not a penny he would give him to waste on pastime."

From Oxford he passed to New Inn and Lincoln's Inn, whence he emerged an utter barrister, but also a confirmed humanist. He had both fulfilled and defeated his father's strictest requirements, as he showed when he accepted in 1501 the invitation of Grocyn to read a course of lectures in Grocyn's church, St Lawrence Jewry—the parish church of his father, John More—on the *De Civitate Dei*. Whether any earlier example of such a reading by a layman in a City church can be cited I do not know, but it is safe to venture the opinion that none had done it at the age of twenty-three.

One sees here the hand and influence of John Colet, who, since More had come down from Oxford, had returned from Italy and made himself felt by the new spirit he introduced into theological study. In his departure from the traditional methods of scholastic interpretation and in his zeal for a reform of the spirit as well as the letter of doctrinal teaching Colet had in More a devoted admirer. He was an outspoken and intrepid reformer, of strict but humane principles, a shrewd idealist, one of the thinkers of the time to whom More was indebted for some of the many criticisms of contemporary life that we find in his *Utopia*. Thus in his *Exposition of Romans* we read that " the law of nations is the law of our corrupter Nature ; a law which has brought in ideas of *meum* and *tuum*, that is, of property and robbery; ideas clean contrary to a good and unsophisticated nature, for that would have a community in all things." To Colet the most disadvantageous peace is to be preferred to the justest war, nor was More himself more emphatic about the perversity of the legal mind and the futility of penalising the ignorant and irresponsible. As Hythlodaye puts it, " We first make thieves and then punish them." The two men had more in common than merely their views and aspirations. In both there was a certain stubbornness of temper and inflexible self-control, and these qualities sprang in both men from simple religious conviction and experience which to Erasmus appeared to have in it something of superstition.

Erasmus' first visit to England in 1499 was an event of supreme importance both to himself and More. If the zeal and austerer virtues of Colet awoke a response in More, so too did Erasmus' avidity for the humanities, his liberal scholarship, his reckless and witty satire, and his hatred of pedantry. But before his return in 1505 More was much in the company of a third scholar, the man whom Colet secured later to be the first High Master of the school he founded in St Paul's Churchyard, William Lilly, author of the famous grammar. The two meditated the serious step of taking priest's orders. They appear to have lived together for some time within the precincts of the Charter-house. The expression which More applies to Lilly, *clarissimus mearum rerum socius*, seems to refer to something more than common tastes and pursuits, though they were associated in a joint translation of Greek epigrams. In a charming letter to Colet, who was in the country, More gives us a pretty picture of his associates at this time. "Do come back," he writes, "though here in town the expanse above is cut off not by the horizon, but by house tops. In your absence Grocyn is the sole director of my life, Linacre is my tutor in study, and my concerns, all of them, I share with dear Lilly."

Yet all along it has been obvious that More was not to become a recluse. We are told by Cresacre More that "when More determined to marry he proposed to himself for a pattern in life a singular layman, John Picus, Earl of Mirandula, . . . whose life he translated and set out." More's interest in Pico was probably derived through Colet. The facts of Colet's Italian journey are obscure, but Lupton seems to be fairly confident that he stayed in Florence and may have come under Savonarola's influence. He may well, indeed, have been in the city in 1495 at the time of Pico's death. If so, one can well understand More's interest in the astonishing young humanist who had invited to Florence the fiery preacher who was to attempt to set up a strictly ordered Christian state—a Christian theocracy in which private interests should be sacrificed to the common good, and in the hearts of whose citizens God should reign. Pico died on the eve of this experiment, and More's life of him makes no reference to Savonarola's theocratic scheme. What appealed to More in Pico was his resolution of the conflicting claims of scholarship, affairs, and the religious life. The little work is dedicated to " his beloved sister in Christ Joyeuce Leigh," [1] who, I find from her mother's will (1507), was a nun of the Minoresses of Aldgate. The *Life of Pico* belongs, I think, to the close of More's Carthusian days.

[1] Joyce Leigh's brother was Edward Leigh, later Archbishop of York, a critic of Erasmus' New Testament. The Leighs and the Mores were fellow-parishioners.

He emerged from the comparative seclusion of his chamber-fellowship with Lilly in the Charterhouse to fall into trouble as a Member of Parliament in 1504 for opposing—" a beardless boy "—an exorbitant demand of Henry VII ; wherefore his father was imprisoned and fined. A year later (1505) he married Jane Colt, of Netherhall in Essex, and when Erasmus visited the young householders in the first year of their married life the two Hellenists interested themselves in translating Lucian. Erasmus has left in his *Colloquies* an amusing but significant picture of More and Jane Colt, which Mr P. S. Allen has identified for us. Erasmus writes as follows :

A young gentleman married a maiden of seventeen years who had been educated in the country and who, being inexperienced, he trusted to form easily in manners to his own humour. He began to instruct her in literature and music, and by degrees to repeat the heads of sermons which she heard, and generally to acquire the accomplishments he wished her to possess. Used at home to nothing but gossip and play she at length refused to submit to further training and when pressed about it threw herself down and beat her head on the ground as though she wished for death. Her husband concealed his resentment and carried her off for a holiday to her home. Out hunting with his father-in-law he told his troubles and was urged to use his authority and beat her. He replied that he knew his power but had much rather that she were persuaded than come to these extremities. The father seized a proper moment and looking severely on the girl told her how homely she was, how disagreeable, and how lucky to have a husband at all ; yet he had found her the best-natured man in the world, and she disobeyed him. She returned to her husband and threw herself on the ground saying, " From this time forward you shall find me another sort of person." She kept her resolution, and to her dying day went readily and cheerfully about any duty, however simple, if her husband would have it so.[1]

---

[1] John Colt's confidence in More is shown in his will, drawn up (1521) ten years after his daughter's death. He left ten marks a year to " Sir Thomas More, Knyght, to the fynding of my young son Thomas Colt till he come to the age of xx yeres and he to order hym and bring hym up in lerning as he thinketh best." We may also note that to his " son More " he left his best *colt*.

Here we must pause for a moment to consider the translations from Lucian. Whatever deficiencies there may have been in More's Greek when he had finished his course at Lincoln's Inn, his intimacy with Grocyn, Linacre, and his friend Lilly had more than made good. He was probably familiar with as much Greek as he allowed Hythlodaye to introduce into Utopia. But if we picture Erasmus discovering his younger friend prepared in the first year of his married life for relaxation we may imagine how happily Lucian met the situation. Here one learnt how to controvert without heat, how to undermine the entrenchments of pedantry and ignorance by irony, and tease the adversary by raillery into some acknowledgment of the truth. Above all, one learnt to be daring in the invention of ingenious conceits. In a word, here was something that went to the making of *Utopia* along with Plato. I suppose it would be considered most improper to describe the *Utopia* as Lucianic, but I wonder whether Lucian has had as much credit for it as he deserves.[1] But More himself was Lucianic in his mastery of irony, and therefore he confounds the simple. An example may be appropriate.

His sister Joan married a lawyer of the Middle Temple, John Rastell of Coventry, whose father was of the quorum for Warwickshire along with the famous Sir Thomas Littleton. Rastell was appointed coroner of Coventry (in succession to his father) soon after his marriage. More visited his sister in 1507, and in 1519, by way of showing the infatuation and perversity of the kind of man who was attacking the New Testament of Erasmus, he told an amusing story of an incident that befell him during his visit. A certain friar, an old Franciscan, had won a remarkable following in the city by urging the efficacy of

[1] The dialogues and declamations that More published were the *Tyrannicide* (Henry VII was on the throne), the *Liar*, the *Cynic*, and the *Necromantia*.

Our Lady's Psalter. More had hardly alighted when the question was put to him whether a man could possibly be damned who read Our Lady's Psalter daily. More's retort that it was " an easy way to heaven " did not suffice. He was asked out to supper, and the friar himself turned up followed by a boy carrying his evidences. The question was asked again. More remained silent, but the friar held forth for two hours. Then More replied judicially that though a prince might grant a pardon at the Queen-mother's request, he would hardly make a law granting general immunity to all who should perform some office for her. But the friar was extolled and More laughed at for a fool.

More's anecdote is confirmed in a strange way by the will of Thomas Bonde, who died during Rastell's coronership, bequeathing to the town the well-known hospital at Bablake, of which Coventry is still justly proud, for ten poor men of the two great guilds, " the said ten poor men being bounden every day to say three times Our Lady's Psalter for all the brethren and sustren of the guild." In the same year, 1507, there died at Coventry a wealthy merchant, Richard Cook, who appointed Rastell overseer of his will and be-queathed " one Bible in English " to Trinity Church, Coventry, and another to the parish church of Walsall. One wonders whether this does not suggest a note of Lollardy. If so, it is interesting to find that More's brother-in-law was looked upon by the donor as the kind of man who was likely to see the matter carried through. It would be interesting to know more about this " Bible in English." We know More's attitude toward the " easy way to heaven," but no more than that. It is perhaps significant that Rastell resigned his coronership a year later and came to London.

Meanwhile Erasmus had visited Italy, and when he

130

returned to England in 1509, the year of the accession of Henry VIII, he wrote in More's house in Bucklersbury his *Praise of Folly*, the *Encomium Moriæ*. He remained in England for five years engaged on the great work of his life, his edition of the New Testament and the Letters of St Jerome. His time was spent between Cambridge and London, and he was well befriended by Warham, Mountjoy, and Fisher. These were the years immediately preceding the *Utopia*. The years of Erasmus' sojourn in England coincide in part with More's tenure of an important legal office, as Under-Sheriff of the City, to which he was appointed on September 3, 1510. He was granted leave of absence to join the King's embassy to Flanders on May 6, 1514, and resigned finally to be absorbed in the royal service on July 23, 1518. It was shortly after this that Erasmus wrote the famous letter to Von Hutten which may be called his " Life of More."

More was, he tells us, a man of medium height, of a clear complexion in which there shone the faint glow of health. His hair was dark auburn, his eyes full of happiness: a pleasant, friendly, cheerful face, with a readiness to smile, inclined toward merriment rather than dignity. His hands were a little coarse ; he was careless of his personal appearance, and his general health indicated that he might live long. No one could be less fastidious about his food. His drink was the thinnest of small beer ; wine he drank in a loving-cup, lest he should seem unsociable ; milk foods and fruit and particularly eggs were his favourite dishes ; he had a penetrating but not aggressive voice, and his speech was singularly articulate and deliberate. He did not sing, but he was fond of music. In dress he liked simplicity, and he had no use for formal politeness. Because he held equality dear, and hated the high hand, he shunned intimacy with princes at one time. Of freedom and leisure he could never have enough, yet when need arose no one was more ready to take trouble. His straightforward, loyal nature endowed him for friendship, and in his circle of friends were men of every degree. His chief enjoyment in life was the company of like-minded men, candid and sincere. He was a delightful man to live with. He had a gift for cheering the depressed, and from his earliest days he delighted in jokes. As a young man he wrote and acted in little plays; he amused himself with epigrams and took special pleasure in Lucian. It was he who made Erasmus write *The Praise of Folly*. He got mirth out of everything, even the gravest matters. With women he was full of jesting and fun. He had the philosophical mind. Like the Pythagorean philosopher, wandering through the market and watching the buyers and sellers, no one was less swayed by public opinion, and no one showed more common sense in his inferences. He loved animals, and studied their individuality. He kept all sorts of birds, and had a menagerie of apes, foxes, beavers, weasels, and other rare beasts. His house was full of interesting things. In his relations with women a union of spirits meant more for him than bodily charms. As a young man he took up Greek literature and philosophy, to the distress of his father, an upright man, an authority on English law and in general a man of sound sense, who, to check his son's proclivities, cut off all supplies and indeed almost disowned him; but the profession of law in England was the highway to success, and when Erasmus knew him no professional lawyer had a better practice than More. Yet old men and priests had attended his lectures on Augustine's *City of God* and did not disdain to learn sacred things from a young layman. At the same time, in spite of his interest in Greek literature and philosophy, he had turned with all his strength to preparing himself for the priesthood. He had almost embraced this ministry, but, being unable to master the desire for a wife, he made his choice. " He married a young girl of good family, who had been brought up in her parents' home in the country; choosing her yet undeveloped that he might more readily mould her to his tastes. He had her taught literature and trained her in every kind of music. She was just growing into a charming life's companion for him when she died," leaving him with four children. To secure the welfare of his children he married a widow of a London citizen, whom he trained to compliance by his buoyant gaiety. With the same gaiety and charm he ruled his whole household. Money had no charms for him. When his household was provided for, and the well-being of his children secured, he spent freely. In his legal practice he thought more of the advantage of his clients than his own. He was much beloved in the City. Indeed, he had resolved to be content with his position there, but his sound conduct of business on embassies made that impossible. Henry VIII *dragged* him to Court—'dragged' is the only word. He had a genius for arbitration, yet no one ever induced him to accept a present. It was their common studies that brought More and Erasmus together. His first years were given to poetry; then for a long time he experimented to acquire a flexible prose style. He took special pleasure in paradoxical themes, because they supplied a keener exercise for ingenuity. Thus while he was still a young man he worked upon a dialogue in which he maintained Plato's principle of community in all things, even in wives. In order to see what progress he had made he invited Erasmus to complete with him and reply to Lucian's *Tyrannicide*. His purpose in the *Utopia* was to show whence evils spring in states, but he modelled it on his knowledge of the English Constitution. No one was happier at impromptu speaking. He was a man of true piety; his religious practices were definite and regular; when he spoke of the world to come you could see that he was speaking with assurance.

I have given the foregoing picture of More at some length, because it describes the man as Erasmus had come to know him during his four visits to England between 1499 and 1516: and particularly during his lengthy sojourn here in the five years from 1509 to 1514. The Lutheran revolt had not broken out when Erasmus carried off More's *Lucian* for Froben to print at Basel. Of Von Hutten, at whose request Erasmus had drawn this portrait of More, this only need be said: that he was in part at least the author of *Epistolæ Obscurorum Virorum*, the coarsest of caricatures of the monks, but so witty that many attributed it to Erasmus. I see no reason to doubt that, as Erasmus suggests, it was More's admiration for the satirical wit of Von Hutten that led to the request for a sketch of the author of *Utopia*. That Von Hutten became a violent champion of Luther is only too well known, but in 1519 the Lutheran storm had not fully developed.

Erasmus left England in 1514. In that year More obtained leave of absence on May 6 from the Court of Aldermen to accompany the embassy to Flanders. He left in the spring of the following year, but in the meantime the City had been greatly stirred by the tragic affair of the heresy and death of Richard Hunne. A careful investigation of the facts of Hunne's case will be found in Miss Jeffries Davis' article on " Ecclesiastical History " in the *Victoria County History of London*, where its significance in the story of the Reformation in London is justly emphasised. Hunne was found hanged in the Christmas of 1514 in the Lollards' Tower, where he was awaiting a charge of refusing the customary burial gift or mortuary claimed by the priest of a Stepney church on the occasion of the burial of Hunne's infant son. Many in the City said that Hunne had been put to death, and this view the coroner's inquest upheld. A subsequent inquiry traversed this verdict, and More felt so strongly the iniquity of the verdict given at the coroner's inquest that he resurveyed the whole case in his *Dialogue of Heresies* in 1528. There were other charges pending against Hunne that explain More's attitude. He was the spokesman of a general attack against bishops and priests : he was an open supporter of the heretic Joan Baker : he had, moreover, in his keeping divers English books prohibited and damned by the law—as the Apocalypse in English, Epistles and Gospels in English, Wycliffe's works, and other erroneous books " in which he hath been a long time accustomed to read, teach and study daily." From the point of view of the ecclesiastical historian the interest of Hunne's case lies in the fact that his resistance to the claims of the clergy to offerings was supported by popular feeling in the City, where the whole question of tithes and offerings was in debate. Though the coroner's inquest had found for murder the ecclesiastical court had traversed the finding and *post mortem* adjudged Hunne a heretic. His goods thus became confiscate to the Crown, and his daughters Margaret and Mary became the King's wards. More's brother-in-law, John Rastell, was rewarded for his services in the French war by a grant on terms of the lands, tenements, goods, and debts of the heretic Richard Hunne, together with the wardship of Hunne's two daughters. It is interesting to learn that Rastell had in mind that the two girls would in due time become the wives of his own sons John and William.

The Hunne case, therefore, was exciting London on the eve of More's departure for Flanders, where his *Utopia* was to have its birth. I do not admit that there is any inconsistency in More's Utopian views on religious toleration and his attitude toward the Hunne case. It is, of course, the same attitude that led him subsequently into his attacks on Luther and to his controversial writings. His attitude toward heresy was defined before he wrote his *Utopia*, and he never departed from it; but to this question we shall return presently.

The embassy to Flanders in 1515 kept More away from England over six months, but it led to the establishment of intimacy with Cuthbert Tunstall, his fellow-ambassador, Jerome Busleiden of Mechlin, a collector and bibliophile, and, above all, with Peter Giles, the good friend of Erasmus. The diptych of Erasmus and Giles which Quintin Matsys painted for presentation to More in 1517 ought to appear as a frontispiece to every proper edition of the *Utopia*, for the famous " second book " occupied a good part of More's leisure time while he enjoyed the company of this friend of Erasmus. If he finished while he was abroad Hythlodaye's narrative account of the ideal pagan state, nothing could be more natural on his return home than to set out by way of introduction and contrast the same adventurer's experience of England. But something should be said of More's attitude toward the publication of his book. This has been worked out admirably by Mr Allen. Early in September 1516 More entrusted his manuscript to Erasmus, who was to look after the rest of the business— that is, get it published. Three weeks later he wrote again, showing some anxiety that it should come out soon, and particularly that it should be supported by commendatory letters, not from scholars only, but also from well-known public men. It is interesting to find that he had kept his secret from Tunstall, for he asks Erasmus whether he has yet been let into it. Early in October More received an answer, reporting progress; and in the middle of the month Erasmus wrote to Giles, inviting him to send a preface, addressed preferably to Busleiden, not to himself. On October 31 More again wrote, wondering whether Tunstall and the others liked it. One gathers from this letter that More was distinctly concerned as to what men of learning might make of his communistic state. In the middle of November Erasmus reported that *Utopia* was in the printer's hands, and three weeks later More had received Tunstall's compliments. " You cannot think how elated I am, how I have grown in stature and hold my head higher ; so constantly do I imagine myself in the part of sovereign of Utopia. . . . But alas ! the coming of daylight has dispelled the dream and shaken me off my throne, and sends me back to the daily mill of the courts."

On December 15 he writes to Erasmus, " I am daily expecting my *Utopia*, with the feelings of a mother awaiting the return of her son from abroad." On January 4 Mountjoy had received a copy from Erasmus, and More's period of waiting was over. This brief statement shows clearly enough that More was conscious that this was no ordinary event. If the world now recognises in his little book one of its greatest masterpieces, is it to be wondered at that its author was more than ordinarily anxious as the time of its publication drew near ? Erasmus seems to have been a little dubious about the venture, and it was not until he contributed his prefatory letter to Froben's later edition that he spoke out ; by which time the book had been generally acclaimed by the cosmopolitan world of scholars.

In his younger days, as we have already seen, More took special pleasure in developing themes of a paradoxical nature, which provided a keen exercise for his ingenuity ; and at one time he had worked upon a dialogue in which he maintained Plato's principle of community in all things. Of this earlier experiment in Utopianism we know no more, but his seven months' sojourn in the Low Countries in the stimulating society of his scholarly and friendly hosts must, as it does with all of us when we are under the exciting influence of foreign experience, have awakened all that was keenest and most entertaining in him. That he should be called upon to explain to his friends his view of the state of things in England and to compare it with that which he saw around him is natural enough. And Erasmus is right in describing *Utopia* as an attempt to show whence spring the evils of states. If in his lectures on the *De Civitate Dei* he had distinguished, as St Augustine does, the State or the city of men from the Church or the City of God, it was with the city of men, the State, that *Utopia* dealt. He therefore in nowise handles in it the wider conception of St Augustine that ultimately and in every real sense the true State is the Church. That this was More's central position his whole life is a witness not less than his death. Like St Augustine he felt the demand for absolute authority in a capricious world; the State must merge in the Church, the civil power become the weapon of the Church, legislator and magistrate be but sons of the Church, bound to carry out the Church's aims; the Empire must be the instrument and vassal of the Church. If this is a fair statement of the practical teaching of the *De Civitate Dei* it is none the less ultimately the principle for which More gave his life. With this higher conception More is not concerned in his *Utopia*: he is dealing only with the city of men. His *Utopia* is the criticism of the social and political life of the day, by the Hellenist standards of one who has the shrewd practical instinct of the reformer. He applies in a somewhat Lucianic manner the philosophy he had learnt from Plato and the ideas he had got from Plutarch to conditions and problems that he found at his door. But it is as a citizen of the city of men, and not as a citizen of the City of God, that he takes his stand. There-

138

fore what More may say of religious toleration among the Utopians must be considered as having reference to such religion only as men by the light of their natural reason may enjoy. Impartiality would be a better name for it than toleration. Compulsion in matters of speculation would, of course, be unreasonable; nor, indeed, would it have been possible, had impartiality not been the rule of the Utopians, for Hythlodaye and his fellows to have taught the elements of Christianity to the Utopians. Subsequent history happens to have shown the State developing its control of the social organism, while the Church has virtually been disestablished; but in More's day, as in the days when our Litany took its present form, men could not think of false doctrine, heresy, and schism without coupling with them sedition, privy conspiracy, and rebellion, and attributing all of these evils to hardness of heart and contempt of God's word and commandment—or, as More perhaps would have said, contempt of "the Holy Church Universal." In the epitaph which More composed shortly before his death for his own tomb—his last retort to the heretics— he described himself as "not odious to the nobility nor unpleasant to the people, yet to thieves, murderers and heretics grievous." He saw in heresy a crime against social order, akin to theft and murder. It is no more reasonable to question More's consistency in this matter by the dramatic dialogue of his *Utopia* than it would be to criticise his attitude to the divorce of Henry VIII—the ultimate cause of his death—by referring to Hythlodaye's account of the easy terms on which the Utopians granted a separation. But I am at a loss to know how to think of those who derive any ideals of toleration from More's *Utopia*. Politically it was the most intolerant of despotisms. Even the colonists had to hold themselves ready to return home to adjust or stabilise the population. The individual must subordinate himself to the system. Nor did toleration —at first a modern political expedient—exist in the religious organisation of Utopia. A man who did not believe in the immortality of the soul, in a future life with its rewards and punishments, or held that the world was the plaything of chance, was a man of base mind unfit to hold office in the State, who was not allowed to air his views in public. He degraded man below the brute; for there was a sect that held that even brutes had immortal souls of an inferior kind.

It has not been emphasised often enough by More's biographers that " he solemnly observed both in earnest and in jest to show no change of countenance in anything that he happened to speak." We are apt, I think, to suffer from our inability to keep pace with the brilliant flashes of More's irony. We condemn, for instance, the Utopian use of slaves, but forget to notice that slavery in Utopia was a better lot than drudgery elsewhere, and that sometimes a poor labourer voluntarily exchanges drudgery in another country for slavery there.

The form that this chapter has taken forbids that I should do more than give to his *Utopia* its place in More's busy life. Indeed, I can pass on, leaving my readers in better hands than mine if they will consult Dr Barker's article on the later developments of Plato's political theory in the appendix to his work on *Greek Political Thought*, or Miss Hertzler's compendious *History of Utopian Thought*.

The New Year of 1517 that opened with the publication of *Utopia* was a year of interest. On May Day—the famous Evil May Day—the apprentices of London arose in a violent demonstration against the foreign artificers and artisans in the City, and in quelling the tumult tradition has it that More played a distinguished part as mediator. It is the stirring scene of More's address to the mob that

140

is attributed to Shakespeare in the play of *Sir Thomas More*.
A little later in the summer his brother-in-law Rastell set
out as captain-merchant of the *Barbara* on a voyage to the
new-found lands. His crew mutinied and set him ashore
at Waterford, and it is amusing to find that the trouble was
caused in part by an agitator who had been one of the insti-
gators of the May Day riots and had signed on as a hand on
the *Barbara* to escape justice. On the eve of All Saints in
the same year Luther nailed his ninety-five theses against
indulgences on the door of the ducal palace church at
Wittenberg. But it was not until 1520 that Luther's
breach with Rome became complete, and Pope Leo X
issued his famous bull.

Meanwhile More had been induced by the King to leave
his City office, and had been absorbed in the service of the
Court. His promotions were rapid, but it was at the cost
of almost everything that he valued most. It was some
recompense that it gave him the means to serve his friends
and *protégés*, and advance their fortunes. But his four
children were now at an interesting age. In 1520, when
her father left England for the Field of the Cloth of Gold,
Margaret More was fifteen and John was ten. The education of his children was now the thing nearest to his heart.
Erasmus described his house as an academy, or rather a
school or university of Christian teaching wherein all studied
all the branches of a liberal education. A letter written to his
tutor Gunnell in 1521, when More, just knighted and made
Under-Treasurer of the Household, was abroad in the
King's service, sets out the educational aims by which he
would have his school guided: above all, he would have his
daughters carry their learning modestly. Nothing can be
prettier than the letters he wrote to his children and their
friends as he followed the Court. Most of them have been
gathered by Dr Foster Watson in his book on *Vives and the*

Renaissance Education of Women. Particularly pretty is the following passage from one of his letters to Margaret:

Thomas More sendeth hearty greeting to his dearest daughter Margaret. I will let pass to tell you, my sweetest daughter, how much your letter delighted me; you may imagine how exceedingly it pleased your father when you understand what affection the reading of it raised in a stranger. It happened me this evening to sit with John [Voysey], Lord Bishop of Exeter, a learned man, and by all men's judgment, a most sincere man. As we were talking together and I taking out of my pocket a paper which was to the purpose we were talking of, I pulled out by chance therewith your letter. The handwriting pleasing him, he took it from me and looked on it; when he perceived it by the salutation to be a woman's, he began more greedily to read it, novelty inviting him thereunto; but when he had read it and understood that it was your writing which he never could have believed if I had not seriously affirmed it; "such a letter"—I will say no more—yet why should not I report that which he said unto me—"So pure a style, so good Latin, so eloquent, so full of sweet affections"— he was marvellously ravished with it. When I perceived that I brought forth also an oration of yours, which he reading, and also many of your verses, he was so moved with the matter so unlooked for, that the very countenance and gesture of the man, free from all flattery and deceit, betrayed that his mind was more than his words could utter, although he uttered many to your great praise; and forthwith he drew out of his pocket a portegue [1] which you shall receive enclosed herein. I could not possibly shun the taking of it, but he would needs send it unto you, as a sign of his dear affection towards you, although by all means I endeavoured to give it him again; which was the cause I showed him more of your other sister's works; for I was afraid lest I should have been thought to have showed them of purpose because he should bestow the like courtesy upon them; for it troubles me sore that I must needs take this of him; but he is so worthy a man, as I have said, that it is a happiness to please him thus. Write carefully unto him, and as eloquently as you are able, to give him thanks therefore. Farewell. From the court, this 11th of September, even almost at mid-night.

[1] Or *portague*, a gold coin worth £3 10s. or more.

SIR THOMAS MORE

Of all the villains in English history Henry VIII to me is the hardest to forgive, when one thinks of all the beautiful things he smashed.

One matter that has perhaps been overlooked by More's biographers is the intensity of his patriotism. To illustrate my point we must go back a little. In the French war of the early years of Henry's reign the largest vessel in the English Navy, the *Regent*, had gone down in flames grappled with the French *Cordighera*. The French Queen's secretary, Brixius, wrote some extravagant verses eulogising the part the French had taken in the disaster, and More had retorted in several epigrams which he published in 1518. Brixius replied by a scornful criticism of More's Latin, and he in turn retorted in his *Epistola ad Germanum Brixium* in 1520. Erasmus had to step in to stop the feud. It is this same spirit of jealous patriotism that marks his first encounter with Luther. Henry VIII had responded to the appeal of Leo X by replying to Luther's attack on the Papacy with his *Assertio Septem Sacramentorum*. In this he opposes Luther's view of indulgences, defends the supremacy of the Pope, and reasserts the doctrine of the sacraments of the Church. Luther seized the opportunity of engaging with a royal controversialist. He attacked the King in a scurrilous pamphlet full of personal abuse in Latin and German. The King could not with dignity remain in the arena, and it was left to More under the pseudonym of William Ross to reply with insult for insult on the ground his adversary had adopted. If his flyting with Brixius seems to us a little provocative it is very hard to justify his *Responsio ad Convitia Martini Lutheri* on any grounds of good taste. We must simply see in it an element in More's composition which is generally overlooked. I sometimes wonder what Erasmus had in mind when he described More's hands as a little coarse—

subrusticæ. But More's character rather gains than loses by seeing it whole.

It was at this conjuncture that he addressed his defence of the teaching of Greek and the fair humanities to the conservative Trojans of Oxford, while at the same time he was writing for himself his devotional treatise on *The Four Last Things*.

Wolsey took up the Lutheran challenge with great energy, fighting it through the machinery of the ecclesiastical courts. Unfortunately he devoted quite as much energy to the raising of his great subsidy in 1524, and the City, already hostile to the clergy, their tithes, and their offerings, resisted in secret both his attack on Lutheranism and his demand for money. The dissemination of heresy was chiefly fostered by the importation of printed matter from Germany and the Low Countries, and so strict a watch was kept on the London booksellers and printers that even Margaret Roper was caught in the net of the good Tunstall's Vicar-General. There were then, as now, many who thought Erasmus responsible for the origin of Lutheranism. Margaret Roper had translated his treatise on the Paternoster, and young Thomas Bertelet, soon to become the King's printer, had printed her work without a licence. He was called to answer for his offence, but, as a second edition bearing a full-page cut of Wolsey's arms appeared almost immediately, ample amends seem to have been made. The preface to this little book is one of the prettiest things in the story of the school of More. It is addressed by the young tutor Richard Herd to one of More's nieces, and should be known to all who are interested in the early history of the education of women. They will find it in Dr Foster Watson's little book on *Vives*, to which reference has already been made.

The methods of the ecclesiastical courts, framed originally

to meet the heresy of the Lollards in the days before printing, were now inadequate. The appearance of Tyndale's New Testament in 1526 and the secret importation and distribution of copies demonstrated the futility of the old machinery. Tunstall adopted a new method, perhaps on More's suggestion—the method of instruction by controversy. He licensed More to read heretical books and reply to them. The subject-matter of More's controversial works can have little interest for the general reader to-day, nor for that matter will he find them easily accessible, but to the student of literature they have all the interest that springs from the fact that the form he adopts reflects the methods of the writers he likes best—St Augustine, Lucian, Plato, and, we must add, the schoolmen, all in their ways masters of the art of discussion. For these reasons, though we may not be interested in its value as an important document for the Church historian, we shall find great interest in the *Dialogue concerning Heresies*. It is a Platonic dialogue in which the case for the opposition is stated with no less weight than that for orthodoxy. It is a masterpiece of its kind. It belongs to the year 1528, when More was Chancellor of the Duchy of Lancaster. His second essay, the *Supplication of Souls*, is equally refreshing, but one business begetteth another, and his controversies with Tyndale, Barnes, and Frith are of a different order. In them More makes the irretrievable mistake of answering his opponents in the scholastic manner, point by point as they make them. The form, therefore, is not the playful design in dialogue in which all his best work is cast, but the forthright pedestrian method of his antagonist.

He had now succeeded Wolsey in the Chancellorship. The charge that he violently persecuted heretics to the death cannot be maintained. He fought with the pen, not with the brand and axe. He held the Great Seal for less than three years. The King whom he was serving was himself violating in act and deed the principles for which More was striving. Less than two years after his resignation he was in the Tower, where he was to remain for fifteen months. It is to the piety of his daughter Margaret in the first instance that we owe the preservation of the writings and letters that belong to this period. Their courage, conviction, and simplicity are as impressive as their freshness and wit. He had the most serene and real faith in the world to come, as a place of great gladness. " Farewell, my dear child," he wrote to Margaret on the day before he died, " and pray for me and I shall for you and all your friends, that we may merrily meet in heaven." The works he wrote during his imprisonment are not controversial. Indeed, one would gather from them that the storm was over. They are a great achievement. In Holbein's group of the More family is shown a Boethius, one of the favourite books of the More household. More's " comfort against tribulation," written in prison, is his *Consolations of Philosophy*. It is a cheerful book, cast once more in the form of a dialogue, and not without the interest of playful anecdote and reminiscence. " They that sow in tears shall," to use More's words, " have in heaven a merry laughing harvest for ever."

Joseph Addison, writing in *The Spectator* during Lent on the theme of fortitude in the face of death, has this remarkable passage :

More died upon a point of religion, and is respected as a martyr by that side for which he suffered. That innocent mirth which had been so conspicuous in his life did not forsake him to the last : he maintained the same cheerfulness of heart upon the scaffold which he used to shew at his table ; and upon laying his head on the block, gave instances of that good humour with which he had always entertained his friends in the most ordinary occurrences. His death was of a piece with his life ; there was nothing in it new, forced, or

SIR THOMAS MORE

affected. He did not look upon the severing his head from his body as a circumstance that ought to produce any change in the disposition of his mind; and as he died under a fixed and settled hope of immortality, he thought any unusual degree of sorrow and concern improper on such an occasion, as had nothing in it which could deject or terrify him.

There is no great danger of imitation from this example; men's natural fears will be a difficult guard against it. I shall only observe that what was philosophy in this extraordinary man would be a frenzy in one who does not resemble him as well in the cheerfulness of his temper as in the sanctity of his life and manners.

It is strange after this noble passage to meet the French historian Franck's reflection on the fact that More died with a jest on his lips: "There is in death a sublime majesty which it is one's duty to respect. . . . Gaiety at this great moment wounds us as a profanation." This surely is to treat the manner of More's death as a violation of the laws of classical tragedy; but perhaps Franck was not aware of the words of one of More's biographers which I have already quoted, that "this he solemnly observed both in earnest and in jest to show no change of countenance in anything that he happened to speak."

A. W. REED

BIBLIOGRAPHY

A full and very scholarly bibliography by the late Mr Guthkelch will be found in the edition of More's *Utopia* by G. Sampson, in "Bohn's Popular Library" (G. Bell and Sons, Ltd.). This edition contains the Latin text with Robinson's translation as well as Roper's *Life of More*.

The later development of Utopian thought is the subject of an admirable article in the appendix of Dr Ernest Barker's work on *Plato and his Predecessors*. Miss Hertzler's *History of Utopian Thought* (Allen and Unwin) is a useful compendium. A modern rendering of *Utopia* by Mr G. C. Richards (Blackwell), with a useful introduction, should be noted.

Much the best modern study of More's life and writings is to be found

147

RENAISSANCE AND REFORMATION THINKERS

in Joseph Delcourt's *Essai sur la langue de Sir Thomas More* (Paris, Didier, 1914). The English works have not found a second editor since More's nephew, William Rastell, edited them in Mary's reign. An interesting *Selection* has recently been published by P. S. and H. M. Allen (Oxford University Press) and should become popular. It contains a rendering of Erasmus' *Life of More*.

Of the earlier lives those by Stapleton (in *Tres Thomæ*) and Cresacre More are unfortunately not readily accessible. The best of the modern biographies are those by Sir James Mackintosh, Father Bridgett (*The Life and Writings*), W. H. Hutton, and Sir Sidney Lee (in *D.N.B.*).

Dr Foster Watson has gathered much interesting material on the " School of More " in his *Vives and the Renaissance Education of Women* (Oxford University Press), and the present writer has dealt with the influence of More's circle in the history of early Tudor drama in *The Beginnings of the Romantic and Secular Drama* (Oxford University Press).

VI

DESIDERIUS ERASMUS

ERASMUS produced in his day an incredible amount of literature, and an incredible number of books have been written about him. To read all with due attention is possible only for the student who gives his life to it. Although I have read most of Erasmus himself I have not read all, or nearly all, that even good writers have said about him. That is a serious disqualification. It is not the only nor perhaps the gravest one. I have had no special training in the methods of historical research as applied to the age of Erasmus : and yet except in relation to his age he cannot be altogether understood. I have had to ask myself with what right I am to speak of him publicly at all.

I have only this answer : I am (what Erasmus was) a classical scholar. So far as I am that, my mind has been fed on the same literature and ideals as his. That may be my only justification for speaking of him now, yet I am not afraid that an audience of historians will consider it a poor one. It is no bad preparation for reading an author to have lived in the same intellectual world with him. To do that completely is of course impossible, impossible even among contemporaries. And Erasmus lived a long time ago, in a world very different from ours. Any modern student who found him easy to understand would only be deceiving himself. However, no modern student is in the least likely to find understanding easy. Erasmus puzzled his own generation, let alone ours. It is reasonable to believe that in some ways the puzzle is clearer to us than to them, for, as the Greek proverb has it, " Time that obscures many things brings many into the light." Yet on the whole the shades about him must have multiplied and deepened. I cannot penetrate them; but I have my lantern. I am not too apologetic about it, because I observe that concerning Erasmus historians themselves are sharply divided. Most, I think, are disposed to the unfavourable view, and even the friendlier among them cannot dismiss him without a grave admonition. That, if I may suggest the criticism, is because Erasmus played, or seemed to play, a weak part in the politics of his time; for I have noticed that historians are inclined to forgive anything in a politician sooner than weakness. On the other hand, to me it comes more natural to see Erasmus as the scholar; and, so judging, I find my opinion favourable. You will not blame me for thinking that my point of view is at least equally legitimate with that of the student of politics or theology. At any rate, it was the point of view taken by Erasmus himself. I am content to see him as he saw himself; and as Holbein saw him, with the keen and subtle face intent upon the words he is tracing in his fine Latin hand.

He has been called a coward or little better. It is easy to see why; and if Erasmus had been mainly a man of action the charge might be made good. But he was not, and so the charge must be considered in another light. We must try to see what his purpose really was, and call him coward only if he failed, and basely failed, in that. At best, the accusation of cowardice is not so much an explanation as the refusal of one. Erasmus was an imaginative man, and a genius at that. Really, to call him just a coward is not subtle enough! I waive the argument that the explanation does not fit all the facts, that on occasion Erasmus showed a good deal of courage. But is our case

150

not proved ? say his accusers. Is it not proved out of his own mouth ? Did he not confess that, for his part, he did not aspire to the martyr's crown and that, if he were tempted like Peter, he would like Peter fall ? I find this point so often made by critics that I fear there must be something wrong with my moral sense. I cannot help thinking that, if Erasmus really felt like that, it was courageous of him to say so. Of course, all who are ready to face the stake for their convictions and to condemn Peter for his weakness are entitled to cast the first stone.

The charge itself, however, is not so easily disposed of. Take, what has always interested historians so much, the attitude of Erasmus to Luther. Here, say many of them, was a situation in which a man with sincere convictions was bound to take sides; and Erasmus hedged. It could only have been from self-interest or cowardice, or possibly from a mixture of both. That is the suggestion, and, on the face of it, it seems true. I am disposed to think myself that there is some truth in it. The important issue is, How much ? The charge of self-interest is not usually pressed, since in fact the hesitations of Erasmus merely got him into disfavour with both parties. But the other indictment remains, and demands a serious and reasoned answer. This answer I proceed to develop. But first you will permit me this general observation. The charge of cowardice is based on the assumption that in the Lutheran Quarrel an honest man was bound to take the one side or the other. Now logically, of course, that is a false assumption; but I am not going to use the logical argument. Erasmus might be intellectually convinced (as in fact he was) that neither Luther nor his opponents were in the right, and yet might feel it his duty to fight for the side he thought least in the wrong. He did not so regard his duty. He had another conception of it altogether. What

151

was that ? A very natural one for a scholar, if I am right, and especially for Erasmus. His position in Europe was like that of no other man. He was the representative scholar of his age, listened to as no scholar has ever been before or since. And in return Erasmus was true to scholarship ; his bitterest enemy has not denied that. The duty of the scholar is to expound the true meaning, as he sees it, of the written word. Erasmus did that. If the meaning he found was neither that of Luther nor of the schoolmen, whose fault was it ? People want him to take sides. But how can the scholar take sides ?

For my own part I cannot see any clear answer to that question. No man, it is true, can be merely a scholar without ceasing to be something of a man ; but neither can one be merely a statesman or a soldier without incurring the same penalty. There may be certain rare occasions (I think there are) when an attitude of impartiality does more harm than good. But was the Reformation one of these occasions ? Was it really so important that Luther should destroy his enemies or his enemies him ? Are we not really glad that neither the one thing happened nor the other ? It is surely time for the historical temper to recover a little from the fierce passions of the great controversy and do justice to Erasmus, because, with regard to that controversy, it is becoming clearer every day that Erasmus was in the main right. His criticism of the Lutheran position, though sharp, is not, on its intellectual merits, unfair ; and is in fact perhaps unanswerable.

Nevertheless, it is not always the man who is right in a great question who is most admirable. There is such a thing as a noble error, and one would rather be Don Quixote than the Barber. If the spirit of Erasmus had been more exalted it might not have seen so clearly. For never was anyone less of what is usually meant by a hero. Out of

152

a hundred illuminating passages the following brief extract from a letter to Marcus Laurinus[1] is indescribably typical :

> If anyone cannot love Erasmus for the weak Christian he is, let him feel towards him in any way he pleases : I cannot be other than I am. If Christ has imparted to any greater gifts of the Spirit and he has confidence in himself, let him use them to the glory of Christ. Meanwhile it is more to my mind to follow a humbler, if only it be a safer, course. I cannot help execrating strife, I cannot help loving peace and concord. I see in what darkness even human affairs are involved, I see how much more easily rebellion is excited than appeased ; and I have learned how many are the devices of Satan. Nor may I trust my own spirit through all issues ; so far am I from being able to pronounce with confidence on the spirit of another man. My desire would be for all to strive together to this end, that through the victory of Christ an evangelical union of hearts may be formed among all men, that peace may be preserved and methods of truth and reason be employed to secure the dignity of the priesthood on one hand and on the other the liberties of the people, who it was the will of Our Lord Jesus should be free. Those who march on this goal will find Erasmus heart and soul upon their side. But if any man prefers to create confusion, I at least will go neither with him nor before him. They plead the workings of the Spirit. Well, then, let those on whom the Spirit of the Lord has breathed dance among the prophets with my best wishes ! On myself the Spirit has not yet seized ; when it has, perhaps I also shall be called a Saul among the prophets.

In a quarrel where the feelings of people are deeply engaged the ironical man is sure to be unpopular and certain to be misunderstood. It is very difficult when you have some cause desperately at heart to believe in the sincerity of an opponent who meets you with irony. If you dislike him you will call him a humbug ; and if you like him you will say it is only his fun. Erasmus has encountered both these opinions of him. I do not know whether he would

---

[1] *Opus Epistolarum*, ed. P. S. and H. M. Allen, vol. v, 1542, p. 227.

have been more amused or exasperated if he could have foreseen that he would be included with Luther in a series of volumes entitled "Heroes of the Reformation"; but, since he had so fine a sense of irony, I think he would have been more amused. Let us be on our guard then with this man, and not take him too literally at his word even when he says he is no hero. He had a cause of his own, which was not the cause of the dogmatists and the politicians, the cause of good literature and sound scholarship—what he calls *bonæ literæ*. To that he gave infinite devotion. Call him what you like, in the world of letters Erasmus *is* a hero.

So much depends on the point of view. To get that right is peculiarly difficult in the case of Erasmus because of the man's complexity of nature. Undoubtedly in many ways he produces a bad impression. The *Letters* give us the self-portrait of one ceaselessly concerned with the effect of things on himself and his personal fortunes. Scholarship and Erasmus are one in his mind. No doubt it is in a sense just this egotism that gives the *Letters* their vitality and puts them by the side of the *Letters* of Cicero. But, while one is charmed, one is not always edified. On one point perhaps a good deal of moral indignation has been largely wasted. The begging letters, which at one period in the career of Erasmus are frequent, and are always possible from him, are nauseating enough. Yet he was no worse in this respect than other Renaissance scholars, and rather better than most. That is a poor excuse, but he had a much better one. Even a scholar cannot live on nothing, and the contemporaries of Erasmus were apparently quite happy to see Erasmus work for nothing. The scandal was not so much that he begged as that he was forced to beg. The egotism of the man expresses itself in something quite different from this and something far more disturbing. If only he could have forgotten himself a little

154

more! A man who cannot do this will inevitably seem on occasion a time-server, a lover of compromise, a coward. So these suspicions have fallen on Erasmus not unjustly. But that does not prove them right. A timid man need not be a coward, and a compromise is not necessarily insincere. What I am disposed to challenge is the assumption that, when the great test came, Erasmus lied to his own soul and spun about it a cocoon of fine theories, which he did not believe himself, and which in fact have no meaning.

What then did Erasmus mean, and what is this doctrine of his ? It is this: that men should observe moderation. And as a sort of corollary he adds that they should study the ancient classics. That is the whole gospel of Erasmus, and I am driven to suppose that almost everybody regards it as one of the feeblest ever produced by man. As if one could steer one's ship through the tempest of the Reformation by disregarding the winds and reading Cicero ! Something like that is what people think of Erasmus. But it is a parody of what he meant, and comes from a misconception. The quality which he had in mind was what the Greeks called *Sophrosyne*; and because *Sophrosyne* is the informing spirit of ancient literature he recommended its study there with a view not merely to imitating it in one's style, but also to following it in one's conduct and character. The emotion, indeed, with which Erasmus suffuses the doctrine is Christian; but the doctrine itself is Greek. Only, what is applauded in the ancients is called Laodiceanism in Erasmus. I can see the point of those who maintain that the times in which he lived were no times for that policy of moderation, of compromise and arbitration, which he never ceased to recommend; that the world's ills required a sharper surgery. But I cannot see for myself that the age of Erasmus had less need of *Sophrosyne* than another. I should have thought rather that it had more. But, as it seems to me, people would not listen to the scholar, not because his remedy was superficial, but because it went too deep. It called for a change of spirit on both sides, and both sides naturally found the demand insulting and intolerable.

Obviously I cannot here discuss the full meaning of *Sophrosyne*. But I may perhaps as a student of Greek be allowed to say, a little dogmatically and not quite accurately, but with approximate accuracy, that what it means is not so much moderation as a passion for moderation. That is apt to strike the modern man as a strange or even impossible emotion. Nevertheless, it was just this emotion which created our European civilisation. And whenever civilisation breaks down into barbarism it is only by a passion for moderation that it can be rescued and restored. That, at least, was the Greek view, the very definition of the barbarian being for the Greeks the man who goes to extremes. They thought him a weakling, and they proved they were right by beating and then making a man of him. The whole of ancient morality is based on the conviction that moderation is strength—but moderation at white heat.

Now this is exactly what we find in Erasmus. His love of peace, his hatred of faction and extremism, burns everywhere in his writings. Of course, this emotion may spring from mere weakness of character; I am not concerned to deny that in the case of Erasmus. I do not feel qualified either to deny or admit it. But these considerations have nothing to do with the sincerity of the emotion itself. It is obviously unfair to say that Erasmus was for concord between the factions because that suited his own interests. He was always the man for peace, and used to plead its cause long before his own future was at stake. It is more plausible to say that he identified himself with scholarship and saw that the strife of parties would be fatal to his profession. Well, and if he did, is that so ignoble a fear? He was always ready to acknowledge that there was something more important than scholarship—namely, religion. But he could not see that the cause of true religion was going to be served by the destruction of scholarship. Rather the contrary.

The character of Erasmus is so fascinating that I find it as difficult as other people to drop the subject. I shall content myself with one contribution to the discussion, and even in this I am not wholly original. Not enough has been made of the physical constitution of Erasmus as a key to much in his character. I realise that this is a very dangerous line of explanation, but if it is carefully used it will explain something. There is, for instance, in Erasmus a great deal of a quality which is perhaps best described as petulance. Although at heart a kindly and even affectionate man, he was constantly saying biting things, which he afterward regretted and withdrew. No doubt if you have as fine a gift of ridicule as Erasmus possessed you will find it very hard not to use it on occasion. That is only human nature. Thus, after Luther had made one of those unsparing attacks of his, Erasmus replied that he would wish Luther a better disposition, if Luther were not so well satisfied with the one he had. You could hardly expect a literary man to suppress a retort like that, once he had thought of it. But Erasmus had not always this excuse. And here, I think, is where the physical explanation comes in.

Erasmus enjoyed or suffered an extreme refinement of the senses. We must, of course, remember his century. It was a time when life was in some ways more splendid, but was in most respects far coarser and more inconvenient than it is now. The distress of Erasmus at certain things he describes will hardly strike the modern reader as excessive or even as anything but entirely justified. But in the early sixteenth century, when nerves were strong and sanitation weak, Erasmus must have appeared painfully fastidious. Everybody remembers his account of German inns, because everybody has read *The Cloister and the Hearth*. But in that account there is, of course, an element of humorous exaggeration. If it stood alone it would scarcely be evidence in the matter. But it does not; the evidence is almost everywhere in his writings, especially, as one would expect, in the *Letters*. Carlyle himself was not more acutely aware of every kind of discomfort or more voluble in his lamentations. Let Erasmus be given inferior wine, or let him but smell fish cooking, or be put in a room with a stove and the windows shut, and the world turns dark to him. Nevertheless, he is far from being a morose man. The very sensitiveness which made disagreeable things hurt him so, intensified his perception of what was agreeable. Obviously a nervous organisation of this kind, though eminently favourable to the artist, will constantly betray him into sallies of the spirit, which may fly in the face of any doctrine of 'moderation.' So the practice of Erasmus does not always accord with his preaching. An old-fashioned psychology would have said that there was in him a conflict between the emotions and the will. Well, that happens to most of us.

It is now more than time to say something about the writings of Erasmus. They, in fact, are the evidence I would offer in support of the argument that all his life he kept applying to questions of contemporary interest the lessons he found in classical literature. I have not the least doubt that any classical scholar who reads him fairly through will accept that view. The Bible, of course, in its original Hebrew and Greek counts as a classic. It is no doubt the chief influence on Erasmus, but it is not the only one, and it is not the characteristic one. *That* is the influence of what an older generation would have called the pagan moralists. This influence Erasmus combines with Christianity, as it may very well be combined; and it is this combination which is his special contribution to his age. Historians have generally regarded him as a man before his time, a preparer of the Reformation and the modern world. What has not been sufficiently recognised is that he produced this effect by the application not of new, but of old, ideas. It is only another illustration of the undying power of the Greek spirit to renew, as it were, the minds of men. The Greek spirit, tending to judge everything by its reasonableness, is a permanent solvent of institutions. It had been absorbed to an extraordinary degree by Erasmus. He is far more truly Greek than is, for instance, Winckelmann, whom the æsthetically minded have tended to regard as a kind of reincarnation of an ancient Greek. And that perhaps is why Erasmus finds it so hard to understand religious mysticism unless it is expressed in terms of human reason, and why he combines this incapacity with a passionate interest in ethics. Nothing could be more Greek.

No doubt it is difficult for the modern world to believe that mere scholarship of this kind could produce the effect which Erasmus undoubtedly produced. But there are certain things which in this connexion the modern world ought to remember. One is the character of his knowledge. We make a distinction between literature and scholarship; Erasmus made none. In his eyes the one implied the other. It followed, of course, that he wrote in Latin. That was in any case inevitable if he was to reach the ear of educated Europe. It is in many ways a pity, for his literary skill, which makes almost a living speech of Latin, would have accomplished wonders in Dutch or German. But a regret of that kind is merely wasted and is a little ungrateful besides. Let us be thankful for a scholar who can write in any language. Erasmus at least could do that, and therein lay the chief source of his power. But we have also to remember in what estimation a scholar of his days was held. The first flush of that revival of classical studies which is the Renaissance in its narrower sense was over, but the light was still spreading. To that light all active minds were turning. The victory of the new scholarship was complete; the old scholasticism was fighting a rearguard action, deserted by the Papacy itself. The vernaculars, which in the Middle Ages had been good enough for Dante and Chaucer, and were shortly to prove themselves good enough for Luther and Rabelais and Cervantes, suffered a temporary but almost complete eclipse. Writing in classical Latin became the mode. It became too much the mode. There were people who said that you must not write a phrase or a word which could not be found in Cicero. Erasmus writes amusingly against such people, and he could afford to do so, because he quickly became the master of all who were writing in Latin. His virtuosity in the fashionable idiom is prodigious. He was, of course, a great deal more than a *virtuoso*; he was without qualification a great writer, rather perhaps in spite of his Latin than because of it. The point I am making here is that, just at the time when he was writing, his facility in Latin was a most powerful factor in creating and extending his influence.

But if Erasmus had found no more to say than other scholars of his age he would have charmed it, but never moved it as he did. He had, however, a great deal to say. While others had been content to write elegant Latin as a mere literary exercise Erasmus used his Latin to dissolve

160

a whole system of thought. He did not do this altogether deliberately; he was partly obeying instinct and the
'classical spirit' he had acquired in his reading. And
naturally he did not perceive his mission at once. He said,
though long after its publication, that his first considerable
book, the *Adages*, was hastily put together to bring him
a little money in a financial crisis; in other words, it was a
potboiler. No doubt it was. The book consisted of a
collection, steadily added to as edition followed edition,
of memorable or pointed sayings, apophthegms, from
ancient authors, with a running commentary by the editor.
Here, as in all his writing, Erasmus showed his *flair* for
a subject. The *Adages* exactly hit the taste of the age.
Every one loved a classical quotation, and here was a whole
forest of them. We shall probably always underestimate
the influence of the *Adages* on European literature, because
we shall never realise how familiar they were to all educated
men. We may gain some idea of this from the *Essais* of
Montaigne and be set wondering thereby how much the
Adages may have meant to less original people. The book
may be said to have done its work by now. It never was
much more than a brilliant compilation. It would hardly
claim the attention of the ordinary reader at all if it were
not for its historical importance and, secondly, for its moral
tone, a tone characteristic of Erasmus and destined to
produce great effects.

This note is more clearly heard in a little book which
followed the first publication of the *Adages*. He called it
Enchiridion Militis Christiani, playing on the double signi-
fication of ἐγχειρίδιον, which means both a short sword
and a handbook. It was written at the request of a lady
unhappily married to a military man, who used to beat
her a good deal, and was certain to beat her a great deal
more if he were to discover that the book, intended for

his reformation, had been written at his wife's suggestion. It was a delicate task, but Erasmus performed it, with what effect on the military husband we do not know, but certainly with a great effect on the public. It cannot fall within the scope of this short chapter to analyse the successive works of Erasmus. Nor, in fact, would any analysis give a true idea of the *Enchiridion*; for it is a series of moral commonplaces treated in a manner which is not commonplace. You might as well try to analyse Horace. " You never think of changing your way of life, and yet you pray God to let you live." " The way to worship the Saints is to imitate their virtues." When a man can put things like that, he will always find a response. The effect was not in the least weakened—it was doubled—by the ethical fervour of the *Enchiridion*. Questions of morals are so far from being uninteresting to readers that there is almost nothing else that does interest them, provided, of course, that the treatment is interesting. Erasmus saw to that.

This interest in morals is highly characteristic of the man. It is what sets him apart from the run of Renaissance scholars, who for the most part were interested only in their scholarship. In that sphere, in the sphere of exact scholarship, some of them excelled Erasmus, and could detect solecisms in his style, although they could not equal or approach it. But Erasmus brought his scholarship to the business and bosoms of men. Thus in the year following the *Enchiridion* he wrote an *Oration* for the Duke of Burgundy, which is a plea for peace. Erasmus was not in the complete sense a pacifist, for he believed that some things would justify a war. But he thought that war was a measureless calamity in every case, and in almost every case a crime. In the *Oration*, and in the later and finer *Complaint of Peace*, he developed his doctrine. It was nothing new. The evils of war had been a favourite topic of ancient eloquence, and in these pieces as in all his writing one seems to hear the very voice of classical antiquity. There is a true and, to my mind, a profound originality in seeing that the spirit of the past was still alive and shaping the present. One is apt to regard the man who wishes to apply the lessons of the past to the present as a doctrinaire, and so he is if he applies the wrong lessons. But a resurrection of the past, as history has frequently shown, can in certain conditions prove the most fruitful of revolutions. The Renaissance itself shows that in literature. In philosophy, in ethics, even in religion, no one who understands the facts supposes that the Greek influence is even yet worked out. In this field Erasmus was the great pioneer. It took more courage than some people think. This condemnation of war, for instance, shows that. For it was not merely academic, not merely the complaint of the scholar or the thinker that his occupation is made impossible by violence, not merely the complaint of a follower of the Prince of Peace. It is presented with a mingling of reason and emotion which makes it something altogether different from a literary exercise or a simple cry of horror. When one recalls how much in the time of Erasmus war was regarded as an indispensable instrument of policy, as an evil perhaps, but a necessary and often a highly profitable evil, his reasoned protest against it will not seem a small matter. Every word of it was true, every word of it was needed, and every word of it was an act of courage.

It was not as if the *Complaint of Peace* had been the work of an unknown man. By the time of its publication Erasmus was the most celebrated writer in Europe. He had advanced to this position in a steady progress. The greatest single step had perhaps been made with the *Encomium Moriæ* (*Praise of Folly*) in 1509. The *Encomium* was written in interesting circumstances at the house

of Sir Thomas More, whose name suggested the subject, and to whom the little book is dedicated. It had
a quite extraordinary success. The theme is, briefly, that
it is only folly that makes life tolerable. It is Folly
herself who argues this, but there is just enough in the
argument to give a bitter-sweet quality to one's amusement.
We have, in fact, in the *Encomium* the most sustained
example of the irony of Erasmus. It is not a very delicate
irony like that of Plato, nor a savage irony like that of
Swift. But its comparative obviousness and good humour
rather helped than hindered its success with the public.
The *Encomium* is, I think, the book in which Erasmus
first completely found himself. For irony was native to
his mind. It was not, as some believed, a trick caught
from Lucian. Irony cannot be learnt. It springs from
the contact of a certain kind of intelligence with what is
inexplicable to it in human life, an intelligence which
naturally affects the reasonable and dreads above all else
to be swept away by emotion. The Greek mind is like
this, and for that reason it is profoundly ironical, far more
than is generally recognised. Erasmus had a mind of this
temper, and so irony came as naturally to him as to Plato
or Lucian.

How would such a mind regard the Bible? That
was an interesting question, and the answer to it was
interesting. Erasmus edited the New Testament, with a
Latin translation. It does not in these days seem a very
startling thing to do, but people thought differently in
1517. The Vulgate was sacrosanct, and here was not
only an attempt to get behind it to its original Greek, but
an attempt to correct it as a translation. The new version
did in fact dissent from the Vulgate in some important
points, and the new text might be said to inaugurate the
age of critical scholarship in its application to the New

Testament. But let it be said at once that, judged by modern standards, the critical value of the edition was almost negligible. The problem was far more elaborate than Erasmus dreamed. All the same, it was a great work he accomplished. He saw broadly what was to be done, and others came after him and did it. And that is not all. There were some things he did which the others could not do, which perhaps no other scholar has ever done so well. Let me explain, as briefly as I can, what these things were.

The modern scholar tends to be a specialist. If, for instance, he is capable of producing a critical text of the New Testament he is probably not capable of producing anything else. The task absorbs all his energies. That may be a pity or it may not. But if we are to have the best texts that are possible—and surely those are what we want—there is no alternative open to us. We need the specialist. And clearly it is right that at least some scholars should be willing to devote themselves entirely to one division or subdivision of the field of scholarship. Erasmus, however, was not a scholar of that type. His fabulous industry, his acute and sensible mind, his feeling for style, enabled him to do work in textual criticism which, measured by the standards of the time, was more than competent. But his strength was not here; it lay in what, for lack of a better word, we may call interpretation. What the original *means*—that was the great question for Erasmus. And here his astonishing literary faculty came to his aid. He could explain lucidly and even entertainingly what he took to be the meaning of his author, however difficult. There are some who appear to think that literary skill is an illegitimate advantage which some scholars enjoy over others. That, of course, is nonsense. A certain amount of literary skill is necessary for the interpretation of great

literature, because in a matter of such delicacy to miss by
an inch is as bad as missing by a mile.

Erasmus, then, could not be content with the bare text
of his New Testament. He added, as we have seen, a
translation, and this he further illuminated by a commentary. The modern critical scholar is scandalised by
the free and easy expansiveness of Erasmus, but he can
also observe that it achieved its purpose and even admit
that this purpose was more immediately important than
his own. Every student of the Bible knows how much
explanation it requires for the uncritical reader. What
Erasmus did was to weave together translation and explanation in these *Paraphrases* of his. The result was that many
a reader felt for the first time that he really understood
his Testament. This, as much as the extreme interest
of having the Greek itself, was the reason why the edition of Erasmus made history. He was not perhaps the
first Higher Critic—a somewhat silly term in any case.
Laurentius Valla has a prior claim. But Erasmus brought
scholarship from the study into the market-place. He
found men agitated to the point of frenzy in defence of
their various dogmas and theologies. He said in effect,
" Before we finally adopt this doctrine or the other, let us
see what the Bible actually says." Naturally no party liked
this. It is hard to find that one has built a structure of
theory on a false or misunderstood reading. So the frenzy
rather increased than abated. But you will observe that
in this work of his upon the Bible, as in all he did and said,
it was the scholar that was acting and speaking, and only
incidentally the theologian and the politician.

The greatest purely literary success of Erasmus was
achieved by the *Colloquies*. Characteristically, his object in
writing the work was practical. It is accurately described
in the full title of the first authorised edition : *Formulas of*

DESIDERIUS ERASMUS

Familiar Conversations . . . useful not only for Polishing a boy's Speech but also for Ordering of his Life. It is enough to make the heart of the boldest boy sink. Yet in fact for anyone who can read quite simple Latin the *Colloquies* is a delightful book. It is, of course, more than that. We must, I suppose, reckon it one of the most famous books of the modern world, even if we no longer read it. It has only to be read to be admired. So far as Erasmus had a model it was Lucian. The *Colloquies* are mainly Lucianic in form, and partly Lucianic in spirit. Yet there is a fundamental difference. Lucian—and in this opinion I fear I may come into conflict with my fellow Grecians—Lucian is not a great writer. I am unwilling to admit that I take less pleasure in him than do other people; and if to be readable were everything in a writer, there is hardly any we could put before Lucian. But there is no depth or passion in him, and so I cannot agree with those critics who would put him in the same fiery sphere as Swift and Voltaire. It may be asked, What of Lucian's irony? I answer, a trick of style. True irony sounds a deeper note.

This note one does hear in Erasmus. Let me, for the sake of illustration, take a passage—not one of his famous passages—from the " colloquy " between Charon and Alastor. I give it in the translation of Sir Roger L'Estrange (1699), than which nothing could be more vivid. The conversation between the two devils has for its subject " Hell Broke Loose "; and it proceeds in this manner:

Alastor. But what says *Fame* upon the whole matter?

Charon. She speaks of Three Great Potentates, that are mortally bent upon the ruin of one another, insomuch that they have possessed every part of Christendom with this fury of *Rage* and *Ambition.* These Three are sufficient to engage all the lesser Princes and States in their quarrel; and so *wilful,* that they'll rather perish than yield. The *Dane,* the *Pole,* the *Scot,* nay, and the *Turk Himself,* are dipt in the broil and the design. The contagion is

167

got into *Spain, Britany* [*i.e.,* Britain], *Italy* and *France* : nay, besides these feuds of hostility and arms, there's a worse matter yet behind : that is to say, there is a malignity that takes its rise from a diversity of *opinions,* which has debauched men's minds and manners to so unnatural and insociable a degree, that it has left neither *faith* nor friendship in the world. It has broken all confidence betwixt brother and brother, husband and wife ; and it is to be hoped that this distraction will one day produce a glorious Confusion, to the very desolation of mankind. For these controversies of the *tongue* and of the *pen* will come at last to be tried by the *sword's point.*

Alastor. And *Fame* has said no more in all this than what these very ears and eyes have heard and seen. For I have been a constant companion and assistant to these *Furies,* and can speak upon knowledge, that they have approved themselves worthy of their name and office.

Charon. Right, but men's minds are variable ; and what if some Devil should start up now to negotiate a peace ? There goes a rumour, I can assure ye, of a certain scribling fellow (one *Erasmus* they say) that has entered upon that province.

Alastor. Ay, ay : but he talks to the deaf. There's nobody heeds him nowadays. He writ a kind of a *Hue and Cry* after Peace, that he fancied to be either *fled* or *banished*; and after that an *Epitaph* upon *Peace Defunct,* and all to no purpose. But then we have those on the other hand that advance our *cause* as heartily as the very *Furies themselves.*

Charon. And what are they, I prithee ?

Alastor. You may observe up and down in the courts of Princes certain Animals; some of them tricked up with feathers, others in *white, russet, ash-coloured frocks, gowns, habits*; or call 'em what you will. [Really Sir Roger is rather wild in his translation here, but substantially right, as always.] These are the instruments, you must know, that are still irritating *Kings* to the thirst of *War* and *Blood* under the splendid notion of *Empire* and *Glory*: and with the same art and industry they inflame the spirits of the *Nobility* likewise and of the *Common People.* Their *sermons* are only *harangues* in honour of the outrages of *Fire* and *Sword* under the character of a *just,* a *religious,* or a *holy war.* And which is yet more wonderful, they make it to be *God's Cause* on *both sides. God fights for us,* is the cry of the *French* pulpits; *and what have*

168

they to fear that have the Lord of Hosts for their Protector?—
Acquit yourselves like men, say the *English,* and the *Spaniard, and*
the victory is certain; for this is God's cause, not Cæsar's. As for
those that fall in the battle, their souls mount as directly to Heaven,
as if they had wings to carry 'em thither, arms and all.

Charon. But do their disciples believe all this?

Alastor. You cannot imagine the power of a *well dissembled*
Religion, where there's *youth, ignorance, ambition,* and a *natural*
animosity to work upon. 'Tis an easy matter to impose, where
there is a previous propension to be *deceived*!

This is the true irony, something different from the
undergraduate wit of Lucian. Like all great writing it
does not come merely from the intellect. But to deal
adequately with the *Colloquies* is naturally impossible in a
brief chapter; scarcely in a volume could one trace out
and study its character and its influence. The humour
of the book, its realism, its novelistic quality, make it
prophetic of so much that was to follow. The study of
this is for the historian of literature, but it is not hard for
anyone to form some conception of the power and vitality,
the germinating virtue, of this old manual for schoolboys.

Afterward Erasmus became more deeply involved in the
Lutheran controversy. That in a sense was the tragedy
of his life, and all I can say of it I have already said. I
have tried to show that whatever he wrote was written
from the point of view and in the temper of the Greek
moralists, as he understood them. The lesson he never
wearied of preaching, the lesson of moderation, of avoiding
extremes, is nothing else than that doctrine of *Sophrosyne*
which, as I put it, and I think it was not too much to say,
is the informing spirit of all the best literature of ancient
Greece and Rome. It did not seem to him incompatible
with the Christian religion. On the contrary, it seemed
to him nearer to the spirit of Jesus of Nazareth than the
ardour of the Crusader. That raises a point which will

perhaps never be settled, but for that very reason the world will never be able to forget Erasmus. His own life indeed ended upon the whole in failure, for the nations were too angry with each other to listen to him. Nineteen hundred years before him a greater writer than Erasmus said of his own troubled times: "Words no longer bore the same relation to things, but had their meaning wrested to suit the speaker's mind. Inconsiderate daring was the courage that makes a good comrade, prudent delay a fine name for cowardice, cool reflection the caitiff's excuse, to know everything was to do nothing. Frenzied activity was the true part of a man, to think out a safe plan of attack was a specious excuse for shirking. The extreme man was always trusted, his opponent suspect." [1]

That is what happened to Erasmus.

J. A. K. THOMSON

BIBLIOGRAPHY

The bibliography of Erasmus is naturally too large a matter to be dealt with in a note. A long list of books and studies on the subject is appended to Preserved Smith's *Erasmus* (1923), and to this the student may be referred. The foundation of all exact study must be the great edition of the *Letters* by Dr P. S. Allen (with Mrs Allen), *Opus Epistolarum Des. Erasmi Roterodami*, begun in 1906 and still incomplete. It may be supplemented from the *Epistles of Erasmus* by F. M. Nichols. Reprints of the more famous writings of Erasmus are, of course, very numerous and generally accessible.

Of books concerning Erasmus there is no end. The English reader may be expected to have read Froude's lectures, *The Life and Letters of Erasmus* (1894). But he should not omit the *Encyclopædia Britannica* article, which was written by Mark Pattison and revised by Dr Allen. Two American books may be recommended: Emerton's *Erasmus* (1900), well written but somewhat biased, and the book by Preserved Smith, very full and up to date, but suffering a little from the writer's incomplete sympathy or familiarity with Latin scholarship.

[1] Thucydides, iii, 82.

VII

MARTIN LUTHER

IT will be well, perhaps, to begin with a confession of what may be failure. Soon after I had begun to study the writings of Martin Luther certain conclusions began to force themselves upon me. But I note with some misgiving that learned students of sixteenth-century thought have come to conclusions startlingly different. I find that Luther is spoken of as a great political thinker: whereas I do not myself find that he was, in any strict sense, a political thinker at all. He has been called a protagonist of something vaguely referred to as "the theory of the Divine Right of Kings." He has even been described as a forerunner of the "religion of the State." I have conscientiously tried to find some sort of justification for these high-sounding terms, and I must confess that I have not succeeded. It seems to me that the character of Luther's political conceptions has often been gravely misunderstood and that his influence upon political thought has been both misrepresented and grossly exaggerated. With whatever misgivings, I can but try to present the facts as I see them.

I must begin with a few general assertions concerning Luther himself. Obviously the best evidence, or the only evidence, we have of the character of his thought consists in his writings. They, it will hardly be disputed, prove this at least: that he was not in any sense, on any subject, a systematic thinker. Patience and coolness are the primary necessities for systematic thinking, and Luther was hot and impatient. He felt more than he considered, and on the whole knew better what he did not believe than what he believed. All his books are *livres de circonstance*; they are items in an excited controversy. He was always an improviser; and was always, I think, sincere in his utterance. So strongly did he believe what, at the moment, he was saying, and so important did it seem to him, that he habitually exaggerates. I am inclined to say that no humbug would have been so inconsistent as was Luther.

The world, I think, presented itself to Luther in two quite different aspects. He never succeeded in reconciling his perceptions, and wavered between two points of view. His most profound convictions were those he shared with the later mediæval mystics. He declared that he had learned from the *Theologia Germanica* "more of what God and Christ and man and all things are" than from any other writings save those of St Augustine and the Bible. But his deepest convictions clashed continually with his practical sense of what was immediately needed to secure the establishment of a reformed Church or of reformed Churches. It may be said of him that, in the long run, he sacrificed his deepest convictions to mere 'practical' politics. "Luther," said Caspar Schwenckfeld, "has brought us up out of the land of Egypt and left us to perish in the wilderness." But at least he did not himself see that he was doing that. His incoherence arose from the fact that he honestly held beliefs he could not reconcile.

By some writers much has been made of a change supposed to have taken place in Luther's views after 1525. I do not think that any profound or important change occurred except on one point; and even there it was not complete. He was preaching the duty of obedience to constituted authority as emphatically before 1525 as after; after that year there appears only a more exclusive insistence

172

on it.   There is, after that year, more stress on the rights of rulers, less on Christian liberty and the need of resistance; more on the need of order and less on the priesthood of man. That this change was due to his desire to strengthen the hands and to allay the fears of friendly princes there can be no doubt.   But it was a change of stress and not a change of view.

One important respect there is in which his views do seem to have altered.   He started his career as a reformer with a conception of 'faith' that he may have derived from Catholic mysticism.   By the 'faith' that justifies he seems, at first, to have meant an intimate sense of the presence and love of God, bringing with it assurance of redemption and safety.   It is difficult to be sure what, in those early years, he meant by the 'Word of God.'   If it were not quite *das innere Wort* of Hans Denck, at least he did not identify it with the text of the Bible.   But, later, and after 1530 perhaps ordinarily, he seems to have used the word 'faith' to signify mere conviction of the validity of dogma ; while the actual text of Scripture tended to become for him the only 'Word' of God.   The change was never quite definite or quite clear to himself; but as far as it went it was fundamentally important.   It affected, of necessity, both his theology and his politics.   It was, partly at least, his later conception of faith that made it possible for him to accept, as satisfactory structures, the churches set up in his name.   It was partly this, also, that brought about the change of his views on the great practical question of toleration.

From these preliminary considerations I turn to an attempt to summarise the content of Luther's political thought as it appears in his writings.   As soon as one sets out to do this it becomes apparent that, except by un-avoidable implication, Luther never dealt at all with any problem of political thought save so far as circumstances forced him to do so. He never thought in terms of the State at all.

Logically as well as chronologically Luther may be said to have begun with a sweeping negative. In the three great treatises of 1520 he not only utterly rejected the claims of the Papacy, but asserted that no coercive power belongs rightly to the Church as such, that the clergy are mere subjects like other people and have no claim to special privilege, and that the whole body of canon law is invalid. From these negative declarations certain consequences necessarily followed. Of the two sets of magistrates, civil and ecclesiastical, theoretically governing a united Christendom, the latter was in Lutheran theory abolished, the former survived alone. At a blow Christendom was resolved into a group, if not of states in the full sense, at least of territorial magistracies, independent and secular. The civil magistrate became at once the only guardian of law and order and the only power that could undertake a legal and official reformation of the Church.

Two remarks may be made before going farther. In the first place, highly suggestive as it was, there was nothing whatever that was new about this assertion, unless, perhaps, the crudity with which it was made. That no coercive power belongs rightly to the Church had been asserted in the *Defensor Pacis* nearly two hundred years earlier. Luther seems to have read that work; but, whether or no he had actually read Part I of it, he never shows the least symptom of having understood it. If he had understood it he would assuredly have been shocked.

In the second place, this declaration that no coercive power properly belonged to the Church, and that canon law is not binding on anyone, was only what was made by all the early Protestant reformers, and was one they could hardly avoid making. It was clear from the outset that no General Council that could be got together would be of any use to them. The only General Council that could conceivably have helped them would have been a Council of Protestant Churches. In 1520 there were no Protestant Churches. The only possible allies of the Protestant reformers were the secular Governments. The assertion that coercive authority rests solely with them simply had to be made; and as a matter of course it was made. But the making of it involved, for Luther, no theory of State right. The assertion was simply to the effect that the claims of the Pope and clergy were based on nothing but imposture and superstition. It was a mere negative. It is, of course, true that later on the claims of the *sacerdotium* were revived, in an altered form, by Calvinism. The earlier reformers simply denied them.

But in all very general statements lurks exaggeration. The early Protestants were not, in fact, clear that the civil power, released from papal control, was not still in some sense subject to the Church. They tended to hold to the notion of a Church having power to distinguish truth from error and declare the truth authoritatively. " This power," Luther wrote in 1520, " the Church certainly has: that she can distinguish the Word of God from the words of men. . . . The mind pronounces with infallible assurance that three and seven are ten and yet can give no reason why this is true, while it cannot deny that it is. . . . Even such a perception is there in the Church, by the illumination of the Spirit, in judging and approving of doctrines." The difficulty for the early Protestants was to say what or where the Church is. There was no idea in their minds of a State independent of any form of religion.

Beginning with these negative assertions Luther soon had to go farther. As soon as he had made them he found himself, as it were, face to face and alone with mere secular authority. He did not need to concern himself with the precise nature or derivation of that authority; and he never did concern himself with any question on the subject. But he was very much concerned with actual principalities and powers and their possible or probable modes of action, and with one special aspect of his own relation to them. There was just one question of politics that circumstances compelled all the early reformers to answer. It concerned their own duty in a perilous position. "We," they put it, "who have the truth, who desire to live and to worship according to God's Word and to order the Church in accordance with the Scriptures, are regarded as heretics and treated as criminals. What is our duty in relation to the civil magistrates, who persecute us and contemn the Word of God?"

No sort of answer, however evasive, could be given to this question that did not involve some sort of theory of civil authority. The fact to be noted here is that all the early reformers gave the same answer, even though it had not for all of them quite the same meaning. They all, with one accord, proclaimed an all but unqualified duty of obedience to any and every regularly constituted authority. You must, of course, obey God rather than man: no one in the sixteenth century so much as suggests the contrary. But, though you may be justified in refusing to obey commands clean contrary to the law of God, you cannot be justified in seeking to save yourself from punishment by any kind of forcible resistance. At most, you will be justified in flight. For armed rebellion there is no justification in any case whatever.

It is important, at this point, to observe that almost all the Protestant reformers assumed from the first that it was necessary to set up formal and visible 'Churches,' with an

176

official ministry, an official creed or 'confession,' a defined system of government. Their desire was, literally, to reform the Church. They desired to destroy, more or less completely, the actual organisation and the doctrinal system of the papal Church ; but, for all that, the idea of the Church dominated their minds. It existed for them, always, as a fact visible or invisible. They seem to have associated religion absolutely with the idea of a visible Church and earthly authority. When they discovered that it was not possible to set up a renovated Church for all Christendom they became resolved to organise local Churches. But without the co-operation of the civil power they could not reasonably hope to do so. There were, of course, dissenters among them. Caspar Schwenckfeld denied that it was possible, in the actual circumstances, to establish any true visible Church. He desired only the spread of the invisible Church, constituted by those who had received the inward baptism of the Spirit and become new men. But the mass even of the "Anabaptists" endeavoured to organise a formal and visible Church. The idea that obedience to the civil magistrate is a religious duty, that is, a duty to God, and that forcible resistance to him is in no case justified, was as old as Christianity. It is, nevertheless, a striking fact that all the early Protestants make this assertion. I do not think it difficult to see why they did so. They themselves said that they found the doctrine in the Scriptures ; but, later on, other Protestants found there doctrines very different. But on the one hand was the consciousness of the perilous pass into which they had come, of the peril of their cause ; on the other was the hope of support from those constituted authorities they could not but fear. The one thing they could not afford to do was to antagonise the secular power. They followed the line of least resistance at the moment. I am not suggesting any conscious insincerity. But the subsequent history of Protestantism in the sixteenth century seems to prove that everywhere and always the attitude of Protestants toward the civil authority was determined by their particular circumstances.

Luther's answer to the question of the duty of subject to ruler was merely that which was given by all Protestants, save a few fanatics, down to the time of the Magdeburg treatises of 1550. From 1520 onward his language on the subject was less emphatic than Tyndale's and not so lucidly explicit as Calvin's; but it was clear enough. Luther was, in his way, a patriotic German. He was hoping, in 1520, for the establishment of a national German Church, freed from the Pope and united under the Emperor and the Bible. But, from 1521 onward, the attitude of Charles V made it clear that no such construction was possible. Thenceforward Luther could see in Germany only a chaos of conflicting claims and jurisdictions. In theory he greatly simplified that confusion by eliminating the claims of bishops and monasteries and chapters and clergy generally. There remained a multitude of 'magistrates,' of various degrees, in more or less indefinite relation to each other and to the Emperor. So far as he thought politically, Luther thought only of Germany. On the question of the legal relation of magistrates of the Empire one to another he always spoke with great caution or refused to speak at all. It may perhaps be held, he told the Elector of Saxony in 1530, that princes of the Empire have, in certain cases, a legal right to resist the Emperor by force; but all that he is certain of is that no true Christian can set himself so to oppose his ruler, be he good or evil, but will rather suffer all manner of injustice. The Scriptures speak quite plainly. God has commanded obedience to magistrates in all things lawful by the law of God and has forbidden active resistance in any case and

178

for any cause. The inferior magistrate must obey his superior; the duty of the common man is simply to obey the magistrate. "God Almighty has made our princes mad"; but he has ordered us to obey them; and whoso resisteth shall receive damnation. It is not a question of how magistrates came to be where they are. Luther insists simply that God has commanded obedience to such magistrates as there are. Simply because this is so and for no other reason whatever, we must regard our magistrates, good or bad, as set over us by God. "I will side always," he declared in 1520, "with him, however unjust, who endures rebellion and against him who rebels, however justly." To plead rights in the face of God's plain command is impious as well as illogical.

The command of God is all-sufficient; but Luther saw two good reasons for the command. If it should once be admitted, he wrote to the Elector of Saxony, that men have a right to resist their ruler whenever their ruler do wrong, "there would remain neither authority nor obedience in all the world." Herr Omnes cannot truly distinguish between right and wrong and is given to striking passionately, at random. But, further, Luther's deepest conviction on this matter was that force and violence can never be a real remedy for anything. He expressed himself in that sense again and again. Rebellion is not only a breach of God's express commandment; it is foolish also and worse than futile. The mass of men are real Christians in no sense, and to rebel or to assert a right to rebel is merely to give increased opportunity to the wicked. Nothing is so satisfactory to the devil as civil commotion and conflict. No good can come of it; and in the infernal turmoil it is the innocent, and not the guilty, who suffer. The Word of God needs not man's weapons, and God is always on the side of right. If you have faith you will be content in that knowledge, and in quietness and confidence shall be your strength. You will, quite simply, obey God's Word, knowing that to use violence is but adding evil to evil.

But, simple as the view expressed seems to be, it was not quite so simple as it seems. Up to 1525, at all events, Luther was as conscious of the need of insisting on the duty of passive, as on the wickedness of active, resistance. The principle that we must always obey God rather than man covered, for Luther, a formidable array of cases and occasions. In the treatise *Von Weltlicher Uberkeyt*, published at Wittenberg in 1523, which contains the most complete exposition of his political views that he ever made, he is largely occupied in asserting divinely established limits to all human authority. If, after the Peasants' Revolt, he was more concerned to emphasise the Christian's duty of submission, that was only because it seemed to him that the times required him to do so.

He asserts, with the utmost emphasis, that the civil magistrate has no authority at all in relation to Christian conscience and belief. It is for him to reform the Church; but it is not for him to say what men shall believe or how they shall worship. That can be settled only by reference to the Scriptures. "The temporal regiment has laws that reach no farther than body and goods and what mere earthly things there are besides. For over souls God neither can nor will allow that anyone rule but Himself only." Only a fool, indeed, would claim such authority. "For no man can kill a soul nor give it life nor send it to heaven or to hell."

Princes, he declares, are "commonly the greatest fools or the worst scoundrels upon earth." And though evil must not be forcibly resisted, yet "one must not serve nor follow nor obey it with one foot or one finger." If your prince command you to believe this or that, or to put away your Bibles, "you shall answer that it becometh not Lucifer to sit next to God. Dear Lord (you shall say), I owe you obedience in body and goods; command me in the measure of your earthly authority, and I will obey. But if you would take away my belief and my Scriptures, then will I not obey. . . . And if, for that, he take away your goods and punish your disobedience, be happy and thank God that you are worthy to suffer for His Word's sake. Let him rage, the fool! he will find his judge."

But there is far more than this. The duty of obeying God rather than man limits the rights of the civil magistrate only incidentally. For Luther the limitations of rightful authority arose essentially from the nature of law. We are apt to be misled when we find some one in the sixteenth century asserting that there is no justification for any kind of active resistance to constituted authority. We have come to associate the idea of political authority with that of a law-making power. That association hardly existed for Luther.

In Luther's view human law and government are only requisite because men are not Christians. True Christians, he says, need no temporal power to rule them: it is the temporal power that needs them. The function of the civil magistrate is mainly the administration and enforcement of a law that, for the most part, exists unalterably. Customary or Imperial law, all merely man-made law, is binding only so far as it conforms to two other systems: to the law of God expressed in the Scriptures and to the law of God expressed in what Luther calls *naturlich Recht*. This strictly mediæval conception is the groundwork of all Luther's thought on government. Absolute obedience is due to the magistrate in the exercise of his proper function, and active resistance is forbidden in all cases. But refusal to obey is justified by any contravention of the law of God, which includes the " law of nature." And the law of nature has its voice in the human conscience. Luther does not deny that a human power to make law exists, in a secondary sense. Law consists essentially in the Scriptures and in the conscience of man. But the precepts and principles of natural and of Scriptural law alike require adjustment to a complex of circumstance. Hence arises the necessity for a *jus potivum*. All the same, Luther was impatient and suspicious of all mere man-made law; and almost as much as the canon law did he dislike the *Corpus Juris Civilis*. Law may be necessary, he admitted; but he was sure there was far too much of it. The mass of man-made law, with its definitions, its subtleties, its technicalities, seemed to him useless or worse than useless. For the right judging of disputes among men, he declared, only a good conscience and love and reason are wanted. " If a judge have love and wisdom, law-books are worse than useless to him. . . . But without love and natural right [*Naturrecht*] you will never be in accord with the Will of God, though you have devoured the Jurists and all their books." It is vastly better, he declared, to appoint good judges than to make laws, however good. " All cases should be decided by natural justice."

The assertion that Luther exalted the secular state seems to me completely erroneous. Only in the most limited sense did he recognise the State at all. He had no sort of theory of state-right, nor had he any conception of a sovereign law-making power. The State was, for him, an accidental result of God's command to obey magistrates. By that command, since the jurisdictions of magistrates are territorial, the territorial state was created It exists, it is true, for the sake of peace and order; but it was not the need of order that created it. It was created simply by God's command, and that command was, it seems, given only because men are wicked. Luther seems to me to have had no conception of the State except as a group or system of governing 'magistrates.' The prince is generally a fool or a rascal; but obedience is due to him. His authority is limited by the law of God; that is, by the text of Scripture and by natural law. But he must not be forcibly resisted. Rebellion is forbidden by Scripture, and violence is never a remedy. On the other hand, of man-made law the less the better. We all know what is right, and where we cannot see the Scriptures will guide us. "Love needs no law," and if we were all Christians we should need neither law nor prince. I think Luther was about as far as it is possible to be from a 'religion of the state.' The religion of the state is for those who have no other.

From 1520 onward Luther was teaching that it is the duty of the secular magistrate to undertake the reform of the Church. After 1521 he was asserting that every prince of the Empire was bound to do all he could to set up a reformed Church in his own dominions. The question "What constitutes a true Church?" had, then, to be faced. Luther's answer to this question, though less clear and explicit, was the same, up to a certain point, as that of Calvin. Distinction must be made between the true Church universal and the Church visible or external. The universal Church, on earth, consists only of those who know and do the will of the Lord. But no one can know that anyone else is a member of that Church. It is, doubtless, infallible, but it has, unfortunately, no possible collective utterance. But any visible and organised Church that is soundly based on the Scriptures, in which the pure Word of God is preached and the sacraments duly ministered, is a true Church. It is the duty of all secular princes to establish and maintain such Churches. In doing this work of righteousness the prince may organise the Church as he thinks fit in relation to mere earthly and temporal needs. He may confiscate existing Church property, he may appoint to benefice, he may deprive the clergy of all special jurisdiction. All this was taught by Luther with an increasingly emphatic clearness. But there was evidently a difficulty. Since no infallible person or court exists, who is to say when or where the pure Word of God is preached and the sacraments are duly ministered? Luther had no answer to the question. He answered it by referring the inquirer to the Scriptures: but it was just the meaning or bearing of the revelation in the Scriptures that was disputed. Implicit in his teaching was the assertion that his own interpretation of God's revealed Will could not reasonably be disputed. But the point I must insist upon here is that never did Luther admit for a moment that the civil magistrate had any authority whatever in relation to doctrine or to the sacraments. It is not for him to say what is true religion and what right worship. He must take that from the Bible. Luther would never have admitted that to say it is the duty of a Government to maintain true religion is to say that the ruler is bound to maintain any religion he happens to think true. What true religion is may, according to Luther, easily be settled by reference to the Scriptures. The ruler is bound to maintain true religion and has no choice about it.

There remained a question of vast practical importance. Is the prince bound, for the maintenance of true religion, forcibly to suppress false doctrine and false worship within his own dominions? On this great question of toleration, as we call it, debated throughout the sixteenth century, Luther's utterances, taken as a whole, are not merely incoherent,

they are flatly self-contradictory.   Castellion, later, was able
to quote him in support of his plea for universal toleration;
while Beza, righteously indignant at such a use of the great
name, was able, as well, to quote him on the other side.

To the question, considered as a practical one, there
were three possible answers and only three: and, in the
course of the sixteenth century, they were all three given.
It might be held that the civil sovereign was under a positive obligation to maintain true religion by force and use
his sword to exterminate the wolves that threatened the fold.
This was the view taken by Calvin and his followers and
by large sections of the Catholics, including the Pope.
Secondly, it might be held that though the secular sovereign
had a right to suppress heresy by force he was under no
obligation to do so.   It lay with him to 'tolerate' or not
as seemed good to him and to 'persecute' as little or as
much as he chose.   This, of course, was the view that
all Governments tended to take.   Thirdly, it was held,
not by isolated thinkers, but by considerable groups of
people, that the sovereign had no such right, but was
bound to allow his subjects to believe what they could and
live and worship accordingly, just so far as was consistent
with the maintenance of social order.   It is important here
to note that only the second of these positions was consistent
with any theory of absolute or unlimited State authority.
Luther gave the first of these answers to the question;
and he gave the third.   He never gave the second.   His
inconsistency was due to the fact that on this question
of toleration, even more than on any other, his deepest
convictions were at war with his sense of what was practically and immediately necessary.   From 1520 to 1525
he spoke for freedom fairly consistently.   It may be said
that in those years he was claiming a right of private judgment
in religion not only for himself—that every one was really

doing—but for other people. The use of force to propagate the Gospel, he declared in 1522, delights the devil. "Faith must be voluntary." In *Von Weltlicher Uberkeyt*, in 1523, he asserted in the strongest language that religious belief is an entirely personal matter and that to make it a subject of legal prohibitions and penalties is unjust and absurd. " A judge," he wrote, " should and must be very certain in giving judgment and have all things before him in clear light. But the thoughts and meanings of the soul can be manifest to none but God. Therefore it is futile and impossible to command or to force any man to believe this or that. . . . Thus is it each man's own business what he believe; and he himself must see to it that he believe aright. As little as another can go to heaven or to hell for me and as little as he can shut or open to me heaven or hell, so little can he drive me to belief or to disbelief." From this he went on to point out that Governments, by the use of force, can, at most, compel people to say they believe what they do not believe. It is better, he declared, that they should err than that they should lie.

" Heresy," he added, " can never be contained by force. . . . God's word must do the fighting here; and if that avail not, then will it remain unchecked by temporal authorities, though they fill the world with blood. Heresy is a spiritual thing, cut with no iron, burned with no fire, drowned with no water. It is God's Word only that can avail. There is no greater strengthener of faith and of heresy than to work against it without the Word of God and by mere force. . . . For we cannot go about even worldly things with mere force, unless injustice has already been overcome by justice. How much more hopeless is it in these high, spiritual matters ! . . . Though we should burn every Jew and heretic by force, yet neither were there nor will there be one conquered or converted thereby." So

186

MARTIN LUTHER

Luther wrote at his best and at the height of his influence. And again, in his circular of 1524 to the Saxon princes, he declared that even Anabaptists should be allowed to preach freely. " All should preach freely and stoutly as they are able and against whom they please. . . . Let the spirits fall upon one another and fight it out."

Yet, as early as 1523, Luther declared that the public celebration of Mass is public blasphemy and should be put down by public authority. This gross inconsistency was curtly pointed out in a letter written to him by the Elector of Saxony. In 1525, under pressure of circumstances, he began to wobble badly: no one who does not know a good deal about the conditions can realise how severe that pressure was. In that year he declared that the secular ruler must protect his people by force against the diabolical activities of Anabaptists—a flat contradiction of his circular of the previous year. From that time onward to about 1530 he continued to contradict himself at intervals. In 1527–8 he acquiesced in the taking of severe measures against Catholics and Anabaptists. In 1520 he says that every one is free to believe what he pleases, but should not be allowed to teach what he pleases. If a man wish to attack the true faith, " let him go where there are no Christians and do as he likes there." Yet as late as 1531, in his Preface to the Shorter Catechism, he declared that "we neither can nor should force anyone into the faith."

Circumstances were too much for him, and after 1531 he went over almost completely to the side of those who, for one reason or another, believed in the maintenance of pure religion by force. In 1533 he laid down the general principle that it is the duty of the magistrate to use his sword for all it is worth for the destruction of false doctrine and false worship. To that principle he

187

thereafter fairly consistently adhered. And yet, though he seems to have convinced himself that only by the use of the civil sword against heretics and blasphemers could true religion actually be maintained, it seems that to the end he must have had misgivings and inward revulsions. In his very last sermon, preached on February 7, 1546, less than a fortnight before his death, on the parable of the tares, he reverted to his earlier view. It is useless, he declared, to attempt to destroy heresy by force: the tares, even Catholics and Anabaptists, must be left in the field till the last harvest.

I wish to emphasise the point that, whatever his view at the moment, there is just one thing that Luther never says. He says that religious persecution is futile, he even says it is unjust; he says it is necessary, and he says it is a duty. But never for a moment did he admit that it was for the secular sovereign to decide for himself whether or no to tolerate heresy. To him persecution was either altogether wrong or it was a sheer duty. He never quite knew which it was. But in this as in other matters Luther's view was never reconcilable with any theory of absolutism in the State.

I have now summarised all the political thought that I can find in Luther's writings. So far as I can see there is no more. It seems evident that his thought was essentially unpolitical. He represented, incoherently, divergent tendencies in early Protestant political thought, which all found clearer and more complete expression later. He was not a forerunner of the religion of the State, he was not even a forerunner of Bodin; but he was, politically, a forerunner at once of Calvin and of Knox, of Castellion and the Armenians, and even of the Mennonites. There is nothing distinctive or peculiar in his teaching on the duty of subject to ruler. There is really nothing distinctive in his political thought at all, except that part of it which derived from his mysticism: his profound pacifism, his conviction that violence was no remedy for anything, his dislike and suspicion of man-made law, his occasional glimpses of a Christian commonwealth which needed neither law nor magistrate. I must add a few words about his political influence. The question of a man's influence is always a very difficult one. We are apt to forget that one man's influence on another is a very complex thing. There are always at least two people concerned. We are apt to forget that the same word or deed may influence two men in opposite directions. As for the written word, there is a constant tendency to overestimate its power; and this tendency is especially strong among bookish people. It seems to me that there has been a deal of wild talk about Luther's influence and, at times, really grotesque exaggeration. It has been said that "had there been no Luther there could never have been a Louis XIV." I think that even the fascination of epigram could hardly take a man farther from the truth than that. The remark seems quite meaningless, unless we substitute the word Reformation for the word Luther. But had there been no Reformation the Europe of the early sixteenth century would have been quite unlike what it was. Of what, in that case, would have been later we obviously know nothing. Actually no connexion can be traced between Luther and Louis XIV. The development that took place in France was completely independent of Luther. In Luther's lifetime French lawyers were already expounding a theory of the French State far more absolutist and far more coherent than any theory of Luther's. If it had been said that had there been no law school in the University of Toulouse there could have been no Louis XIV it would not have been true, but it would have been intelligible.

Luther's courageous stand against principalities and powers from 1517 to 1521 was potent as an example and as a stimulant all over Western Christendom. It was the interest his conduct aroused and the prestige it brought him that gave their immense vogue to the treatises of 1520. It was in that year and in the few years immediately following that his personal influence was greatest. But it is impossible to attribute to his stimulating example any definite results in the world of political thought. It was certainly of importance that such a man should have preached, with a constant and increasing emphasis, the duty of obedience to the civil magistrate and the wrongfulness in all cases of armed resistance and rebellion. Few, indeed, at the time, can have formed any definite notion of Luther's political doctrines as a whole. But what the common man needs and seeks is merely a practical conclusion and rule of life. In Germany, at least, Luther must have done a good deal to strengthen that tendency to regard rebellion against constituted civil authority as rebellion against God, which, strong ever since St Paul's time, was in the sixteenth century becoming stronger than ever it had been. But facts do not seem to justify us in saying more than this. Everywhere in the first half of the sixteenth century the Protestants were preaching the same doctrine. Even the mass of those currently called Anabaptists taught submission to civil authority. Nor was there anything at all distinctively Protestant about this view. The same conclusion was being simultaneously taught, from a different point of view, in the law schools of France and Italy. It was taught by Bishop Gardiner as well as by Tyndale and asserted as clearly by L'Hôpital as by Calvin.

It is clear, too, that if Luther's influence drew many in the direction of a submissive dependence upon civil authority he must have moved many others in a quite contrary direction. His insistence on the duty of resisting man in obedience to God, his early insistence on natural priesthood and Christian liberty, above all, perhaps, his insistence that a truly Christian community would need neither law nor magistrate, must have drawn many minds toward what is roughly called Anabaptism. Those who accused him, in spite of his emphatic assertions of the duty of submission, of inciting to violent revolution, were not so very far wrong. " I believe," he wrote in 1520, " that there is on earth, wide as the world, but one holy, common Christian Church, which is no other than the community of the saints. . . . I believe that in this community or Christendom all things are in common and each man's goods are the other's, and nothing is simply a man's own." Luther's thought was nearer that of the Anabaptists than he himself was aware.

Luther has been far too much identified with the results of the Reformation in Germany and even in Europe at large. He has been far too much identified with what is called " Lutheranism." His influence in Germany and in the lands to the north of it was great ; in the Netherlands it was considerable, in England slight, and in France it is hardly traceable after 1525. Ideally there is little connexion between his teaching and the systems of government that were established in Germany by the princes he tried to use and who made use of him. He gave his great name to state-ridden Churches along with but small measure of his great spirit. He ought to have known better than to do so : we may say, perhaps, that he did know better, though he never knew it. His life was a tragedy, that he never, himself, appreciated.

J. W. Allen

RENAISSANCE AND REFORMATION THINKERS

BIBLIOGRAPHY

A. PRIMARY SOURCES

LUTHER, MARTIN: *Werke. Kritische Gesammtausgabe.* Weimar, 1883–
1904.
Opera Latina ad Reformationis Historiam Imprimis Pertinentia. Frank-
fort, 1865–73. ,
Briefwechsel, edited by C. A. Burkhardt. Leipzig, 1866.
Briefwechsel, edited by W. Enders. Frankfort, 1884–93.
Die drei Reformationsschriften Luthers vom Jahre 1520. Gotha, 1884.
The Three Primary Works of Luther, translated by Wace and Buchheim.
London, 1885.
Table Talk, edited by Hazlitt. London, 1900.

B. SECONDARY SOURCES

JACOB, H. E.: *Martin Luther.* New York, 1898.
KÖSTLIN, J.: *Martin Luther, sein Leben und seine Schriften.* Elberfeld,
1875.
LINDSAY, T. M.: *Luther and the German Reformation.* Edinburgh, 1900.
MELANCHTHON, P.: *Historia de Vita et Actis Lutheri.* Wittenberg, 1545.
MURRAY, R. H.: *Erasmus and Luther.* London, 1920.
WARING, L. H.: *The Political Theories of Martin Luther.* New York,
1910.

VIII

JOHN CALVIN

THE critical point in the life of Calvin is the year
1536. In that year he published the first edition
of his *Institutes of the Christian Religion* and almost
at once stood out in the public eye as the leading intellect
of the reforming movement. In the same year he took up
his abode in Geneva, from which city, with one short
interval, he was to exercise a growing and determinative
influence on the thought and politics of Europe. It was
by what must seem to the outward eye an accident that the
city of Geneva claimed its greatest citizen. Calvin had
no intention of staying there and no desire to spend his life
in tasks of government and leadership. He was looking
forward to a career of study and authorship in which he
would defend and expound by the pen the divine truth
which he had only lately fully understood. The French
preacher Farel, who was attempting to direct the Protestant
but turbulent citizens of Geneva, spoke then to an unwilling
man when he urged Calvin to share with him the task
which seemed beyond his own powers. The vehement
adjuration with which Farel warned him not to refuse the
call struck on Calvin's mind with the force of a divine
command, and he recognised, in later years, the working
of Providence through this sudden appeal, carrying him
where he would not and to destinies which he had not
chosen.

The man who thus entered upon his life-work was not
unformed. On the contrary, though he was only twenty-

193

seven years of age, the foundations of his character and thought had already been laid, and it was a person of settled convictions and determined outlook who became a coadjutor and soon almost an autocrat in the Protestant republic. Born at Noyon in Picardy, he was the son of an ecclesiastical official, his father being the procurator fiscal and secretary to the bishop. In his earliest years he became familiar with the abuses which prevailed in the old ecclesiastical system, since the see of Noyon was the appanage of a powerful aristocratic family and was the scene of undignified quarrels between the bishop and the chapter of the cathedral. At a tender age also Calvin began to profit by these abuses and, when twelve years old, obtained a chaplaincy through the influence of his father. Partly supported by the revenue thus acquired, he studied in the University of Paris with a view to qualifying himself for an ecclesiastical career. After four years of life in Paris, however, he began the study of law, which he pursued with great diligence in Orleans and Bourges. The change in the direction of his studies appears to have been due primarily to the instigation of his father, who was probably not unable to read the signs of the times ; nevertheless, Calvin seems to have found in law a subject congenial to his mind. We shall understand him better if we remember his years at Orleans and Bourges. The first-fruits of this period of intellectual activity appeared in a commentary on Seneca's *De Clementia*, which gave promise that its author would become one of the foremost scholars of his time. One characteristic of this work, however, leads to the question when the mind of Calvin began to move toward the new views of religion. There is no evidence in the *Commentary* of interest in theological questions ; but it is certain that its author had already come under the influence of men such as Olivetan and Lefèvre, who were adherents of

194

the evangelical faith.   It is clear, however, that shortly
after its publication Calvin definitely abandoned all intention of being ordained to the priesthood and ranged himself
with the reforming party.   The turning-point came in 1533,
when Nicholas Cop, Rector of the University of Paris,
delivered an inaugural address advocating the New Testament as the basis of theology.   It is believed that Calvin
had a great share in the composition of this address, and
it is at least certain that he withdrew to Basel during the
outcry which followed, apparently regarding the event as a
definite breach with the past.

We may thus discern, besides the influence of the
new interest in and understanding of the Bible, two other
formative influences which left an abiding impression on
Calvin's mind.   He was a humanist.   All the greater reformers were to some extent children of the new learning,
but none had perhaps so clear a right in the family as he.
Calvin's most permanent contribution to literature is to be
found in his commentaries on Scripture.   They bear the
marks of one who had learned in the school of classical
studies to interpret the meaning of an author and to consider the circumstances in which he wrote.   And he was
a lawyer.   It is to this, perhaps, that we should attribute
the less attractive elements in his thinking.   His theology
is legal, and his mind is clear rather than capacious, ruthless
in logic rather than rich in reflection.

The Reformation was not like a river which becomes
sundered into two streams at some distance from its source.
There were two streams from the beginning, one rising
in Germany, the other in Switzerland.   Calvin belongs to
the Swiss Reformation.   Though both Zwingli and Calvin
were influenced by Luther, the former was preaching his
new doctrine before any writing of the German reformer
came into his hands, and the latter from the beginning

maintained an independent position. The Reformed Church which has as its Fathers Zwingli and Calvin shared, of course, in the Lutheran hostility to Rome and co-operated in this common controversy. From the out-set, however, the Reformed Church exhibited many important differences from its Lutheran sister. It arose, not as the Lutheran movement in monarchical states, but in republics, and it naturally tended to take a more democratic colour. Closely connected with this is its international character. While the Lutheran movement allied itself with national Governments, and organised itself in state and national Churches, the Calvinist movement escaped this limitation and approached the status of a universal Church transcending national frontiers and opposing to the world-wide claim of Rome a pretension not less comprehensive. During the later years of his life in Geneva Calvin ruled by his influence an ecclesiastical organisation scarcely less united and scarcely less extensive than that which acknowledged the Pope. The difference in spirit between the Lutheran and Calvinist Churches was partly reflected and partly caused by a difference in theological standpoint. The Lutheran theology was less drastic in its reaction against the old system, and in spite of the violence of his language Luther desired no violent break with the past. The form of worship was changed as little as possible ; the Mass in its essential features was preserved ; and, as is well known, Luther maintained a stubborn resistance to any doctrine of the Eucharist which would deny the real presence. The Lutherans had no theoretical objection to episcopacy so long as the bishops would allow the pure Gospel to be preached, by which they meant the doctrine of justification by faith. There was not even a necessary and *de fide* opposition to the Papacy as an institution. Melanchthon declared that he had no objection to recog-

196

nising the authority of the Pope *jure humano*, provided that the Pope did not oppose the Gospel.

" Calvinism was in a sense quite unknown to Lutheranism the conscious and constant antithesis to Rome." [1] These words of Dr Fairbairn are true. The legal and logical intelligence of Calvin could not be satisfied with compromise and uncertainty. He was happy only with antitheses, and his power in the world of the sixteenth century arose chiefly from the fact that he provided the Reformation with a scheme of doctrine as coherent and an ideal of Church order as definite as those of the Roman enemies. To the infallibility of the Church was opposed the infallibility of the Word of God, to the rounded system of scholastic theology, based on Aristotle and the dogmas of the Church, was opposed a scheme of doctrine founded on one leading thought—the sovereignty of God.

Though the Calvinistic theology has real and important characteristics which differentiate it from the Lutheran, we must beware of exaggerating them into a radical opposition. The difference is one of emphasis and order of thought, not of actual disagreement. The theology of the orthodox Reformation as a whole was based upon the assertion of the supreme authority of Scripture, and in this matter Calvin is its true child. It would be a great mistake to regard him as primarily a philosopher working out a view of the world from the starting-point of a principle which he had accepted on purely rational grounds. His teaching is Biblical theology, not philosophy, and is intended to be an exposition of the deliverances of the infallible Word of God. It is interesting, therefore, to observe the grounds on which he accepted this fundamental authority. His position with regard to Scripture is in some respects less modern than that of Luther, who was

[1] A. M. Fairbairn, *Christ in Modern Theology*, p. 149.

prepared to question the full inspiration of some books in the canon. Calvin has no such doubts. He takes the books of the Bible as contained in the Vulgate, with the exception of the so-called Apocrypha, without question. There is, however, a note of a much more modern kind in Calvin's attitude toward Scripture. It is a remarkable fact that he appears to have felt little need to defend its authority or inspiration. His theological position, of course, precluded him from deriving the authority of the Bible from that of the Church. He relies almost entirely on the testimony of the Holy Spirit to the individual. Though he dwells upon the antiquity of the books which compose the Old Testament he really bases everything upon internal evidence. The Bible commends itself to us by its very nature as the Word of God; it is αὐτόπιστος, self-evidencing : when we read it with a pious mind we cannot doubt that it is true and comes from God. It is sufficiently evident that this doctrine, carried to its logical conclusion, would issue in a thorough individualism, since the evidence of revelation would consist in the reaction of every person, taken one by one, to the Bible. Very far from Calvin's intention, however, was any such conclusion, and he had certainly no notion of tolerating those who, having read the Bible with as pious a mind as they could command, failed to find in it the Word of God. Nor, again, does he wish that every man should interpret for himself the divine oracles. No one was more conscious than he of the natural imbecility of the human intelligence or of the confusions and mistakes which must arise from unguided liberty of exegesis. The *Institutes of the Christian Religion* is put forward by him as a clue to the meaning of Scripture, a key to the essential teaching of revelation. Thus in the preface to the second edition he says : " Having thus as it were prepared the way, I shall not feel it necessary in any com-

JOHN CALVIN

mentaries on Scripture which I may afterward publish to
enter into long discussions of doctrine. In this way the
pious reader will be saved much trouble and weariness, provided he comes furnished with a knowledge of the present
work as an essential prerequisite."

From the theological point of view the Reformation
may be regarded as a revival of the religious conceptions
of St Paul and St Augustine. Against the doctrine of
merit was set up again the master-thought of the omni-
potent and infinite God apart from whose grace man could
do no good and in whose presence man could make no
claim. The Apostle of the Gentiles had connected with
this conception a view of history which he derived from
Judaism and ultimately from the Hebrew prophets. In
his vision the course of the world was no chance current
of events, but a providential order in which every turn was
foreknown and foreordained by God, so that even the rejection of Israel was a part of the divine plan for the human
race. This conception of the infinite and sovereign God
is the foundation-stone of Calvin's religion as it had
been for St Paul and Augustine. His teaching is in the
full sense a theology—a doctrine of God. The world is
created by God, and His Will is the ultimate cause of
every event within it. Not only so, but the end or purpose
of creation is nothing else but God. It exists for His glory
and for no other reason at all. The damned no less than
the saved contribute to this end, for if the latter display
His mercy the former exemplify His justice. "The strength
of Calvinism lay in the place and pre-eminence it gave to
God : it magnified Him ; humbled man before His awful
majesty, yet lifted him in the very degree that it humbled
him. Catholicism is essentially a doctrine of the Church.
Calvinism is essentially a doctrine of God." [1]

[1] A. M. Fairbairn, *op. cit.*

The doctrine of predestination, which is often said to be the distinguishing feature of Calvin's teaching, is in reality a consequence of this conception of God. It is clear that a thoroughgoing theory of divine sovereignty and providence cannot remain content with looking on the general tendency of history as the expression of the divine will. History is, after all, made by the lives and wills of individuals, and these too must be brought under the same principle. There can be little doubt that St Paul uses language which, if pressed to its logical conclusion, would seem to deny any real freedom to the individual in the ordinary sense of the words, and which seems to imply the predestination of a part of the human race to salvation. There are, however, other passages in the Pauline writings which convey a different idea, and it is manifestly an error to treat the Epistles as a system of theology. This was, however, the error which was made by all the Reformers, and by no one more thoroughly than by Calvin. The predestination element in St Paul's thought was taken without qualification by the theologians of the Reformation as an essential part of the Christian faith. Calvin is not alone here. Luther in his *De Servo Arbitrio* had seized the same " hammer " to smash the belief in the possibility of human merit. There is no real difference between the two great Reformers on this point, except that Calvin works out the conception with greater clearness and more lawyer-like persistence. It may, indeed, even be argued that Calvin was less extreme in his predestination doctrine than Luther; for the latter, following Duns Scotus, appears to hold that even moral distinctions depend upon the arbitrary Will of God, upon a mere *fiat* without law or reason. Calvin, it is true, speaks sometimes in a manner which might be thought to have the same implication. " What temerity it is even to inquire the causes of God's Will, seeing that this is, and of good right ought to be, the cause of all the things that are. . . . The Will of God is in such a manner the supreme rule and ruler of justice that it is necessary to hold everything just because He wills it. Therefore when it is asked, Why has God done this ? it must be replied, Because He has willed it. If we go farther and ask why He has willed it, that is to ask for something higher and greater than the Will of God, which cannot be found." But these passages do not fully express Calvin's view on the subject. He does not mean to separate the Will of God from the nature of God or think of a bare will. " We do not imagine a God who has no law, seeing that He is a law to Himself." "It is certain that the goodness of God is so united with His divinity that it is not less necessary for Him to be Will than to be God."[1] Calvin's real view seems to be that the Will of God is the expression of the divine nature which itself embraces both the law of justice and the norm of goodness.

The doctrine of predestination is then a logical deduction from the Calvinistic conception of God. It was, moreover, no new thing in Christian theology. In all its essential features it is to be found in Augustine. Attempts have been made to draw a clear distinction between Augustine's teaching on this matter and that of Calvin, but to little effect. Important divergencies between the two thinkers arise from their diverse conceptions of the Church and sacramental system, but fundamentally there is agreement. The words of Dr J. B. Mozley sum up the doctrine and the coincidence of Calvin and Augustine with a clearness and precision which cannot be surpassed : " I see no substantial difference between the Augustinian and Thomist and the Calvinist doctrine of predestination.

---

[1] For these and other passages referred to see E. Doumergue, *Jean Calvin*, vol. ii, pp. 120–125.

St Augustine and Calvin alike hold an eternal divine decree, which, antecedently to all action, separates one portion of mankind from another, and ordains one to everlasting life and the other to everlasting punishment. That is the fundamental statement of both; and it is evident that while this fundamental statement is the same there can be no substantial difference in the two doctrines." [1] It would, however, be an error to suppose that this view of the condition of the human race is equivalent to a doctrine of fatalism. Possibly the position of Calvin ought logically to have led to such a conclusion, but it is certainly one which he did not draw. To make a coherent theory out of his statements about the human will and freedom is probably impossible, but we can at least assert that he repudiated the charge of making God the author of sin as a calumny on his theology. Man is really responsible for the evil that he does. The opposite of freedom, Calvin holds, is not necessity, but constraint. The will of man is not constrained, because it is not moved by forces acting from outside. It is moved from within. But, though not constrained, it is necessitated. The actions of a man may truly be attributed to his will, and he must be considered, therefore, as their author and responsible. Nevertheless, in the man who is not among the elect and whose will is not sanctified by irresistible grace there is no possibility of choosing good. His will, though not constrained, is necessitated, being the will of a fallen being, to the choice of evil. " We agree that man has a will, such that when he does evil he ought to impute it to himself and to the choice of his will. . . . We deny that this will is free, because, on account of the natural perversity in man, he tends necessarily to evil and can only desire evil." [2]

[1] *Predestination*, pp. 393 ff., where the chief passages are collected.
[2] E. Doumergue, *Jean Calvin*, vol. iv, p. 169.

JOHN CALVIN

The reader may well be complaining that he has heard so far nothing about Calvin's political and social ideas, and seems to be presented instead with a theological discussion. If, however, he is a wise reader he will understand that Calvin's theology is really the chief part of what he has to say about social life, and that to expound any aspect of his teaching apart from its theological root is the certain way to misinterpretation. The few pages given to Calvin in the text-books of the histories of political ideas which are now appearing in large numbers are melancholy evidence of this truth. It is to be feared that the students who read these text-books for the purpose of examination gain from them simply the impression that he was a theologian who held some commonplace and rather incoherent opinions about society and exercised a quite incomprehensible influence on history. They would know more about Calvin's position even as a political thinker if they had some knowledge of his theology and knew nothing of his comparatively meagre remarks upon social and political theory. For Calvin's whole thought is determined by his views about God and man's estate. It is, indeed, a misnomer to call them ' views.' In his mind they were the assured and indubitable truth. As Mark Pattison has said, " His theory was not a part of his mental furniture as other men's theories are to them. It was the whole of his intellect. No question had to him two sides. There was but one right reason. All other modes of thought were depravity, not reason at all, but moral perversity." [1] Calvin's conception of life and its conditions is in many respects remote from the modern mind, yet not in all its aspects. The power of a determinist creed has recently been shown again in the Russian revolution, where the triumph remained not with the reformers who talked of freedom, but with the

[1] " Calvin at Geneva."

army which marched under the banner of the materialistic conception of history. Karl Marx is a kind of economic Calvin. But the difference is, of course, profound. There is a dramatic colouring and an other-worldliness in Calvinism which cannot be found in theories which have a merely social aim. We cannot help feeling something of its sombre grandeur. This little life of ours is an episode in the eternal drama. The characters were cast long before the present scene began, and the *dénouement* lies beyond. Meanwhile the actors are playing their parts, which are determined, though to them unknown. The meaning of the present order is to be found entirely outside it, in the hidden divine decrees which are prior to creation and in the final separation hereafter between the elect and the reprobate. Calvinism as held by Calvin is the most extreme ' other-world ' religion.

When we make real to ourselves in imagination the kind of universe in which Calvin lived and thought we can see at once that the questions which have agitated political and social reformers must have for him at the most a subordinate interest. Liberty and the pursuit of happiness in this world could have little consequence for one whose eyes were fixed upon the eternal destinies. Freedom to worship God in accordance with His Will is desirable, but Calvin would have felt nothing but contempt for a man who could find in progress toward some earthly Utopia sufficient food for the life of the spirit. Nevertheless, the social interests cannot be ignored entirely even by the most fervent believer in an ' other-worldly ' creed, and Calvin's life in Geneva brought him face to face with most of the problems of government. As we might expect, however, the organisation of the Church and its discipline occupy a far greater place in his mind than the civil State, and the question with him is not, as it might be with a modern thinker, what should be the position of the ecclesiastical body within the State, but rather what functions does the true conception of the Church allow to or impose upon the State. The duties and privileges of secular magistrates are discussed at the end of the *Institutes*, and the whole treatment is almost perfunctory compared with the elaborate argument of the rest of that work. Calvin is as definitely an ecclesiastical statesman as any Pope, and we shall do well therefore to approach his ideas concerning society through his doctrine of the Church.

Like the Protestant theology the Protestant conception of the Church owes much to Augustine. That Father had drawn a distinction between the actual organised Christian community and the *Communio Sanctorum* which alone can claim to be the true Church. Those who are genuinely members of the Church of Christ are they only who belong to the company of the elect and are saved by grace and predestined to eternal life ; and they are by no means identical with those who are outwardly adherents of the ecclesiastical polity. This distinction has introduced a good deal of confusion into Augustine's teaching, for it is by no means always clear whether he means the actual or the ideal Church to be regarded as the *Civitas Dei*. This distinction, which was only partially explicit in the thought of Augustine, becomes quite definite in the theory of the reformers. The opinion of Wycliffe, *quod nullum est membrum Sanctæ Matris Ecclesiæ nisi persona predestinata*, was that of Luther and Calvin alike, but as the latter worked out the consequences of predestination more logically so he seized more firmly upon the implied doctrine of the Church. In Calvin the distinction becomes that between the Church visible and the Church invisible. The invisible Church consists of those, known only to God, who by His inscrutable decree have been preordained to become

His children by grace. But this true invisible Church requires a concrete organ and is partially manifested in a visible society. Calvin tells us clearly enough what he means by the visible Church. It is " the whole multitude dispersed throughout the world who profess to worship one God and Jesus Christ, who are initiated into His faith by baptism, who testify their unity in true doctrine and charity by a participation in the Holy Supper, who consent to the Word of the Lord, and preserve the ministry which Christ has instituted for the purpose of preaching it." [1] It is most important to notice that nothing could be farther from Calvin's intention than to weaken the claim of the visible Church on the allegiance of men; nothing would have been more distasteful to him than the argument that, since the true Christians are known only to God, a man may safely separate himself from the fellowship of the Christian society. On the contrary, there is only one Church, and it is the duty of all men to remain in communion with her. " We may learn from her title of mother how useful and even necessary it is for us to know her; since there is no other way of entrance into life, unless we are conceived by her, born of her, nourished at her breasts, and continually preserved under her care and government till we are divested of this mortal flesh and become like the angels. For our infirmity will not admit of our dismission from her school; we must continue under her instruction and discipline to the end of our lives. Out of her bosom there can be no remission of sins. . . . It is always dangerous to be separated from the Church." [2] The most rigid Catholic could scarcely desire to strengthen this language, and we may learn from it that the quarrel between Calvin and Rome had nothing to do with any attempt to lighten the pressure of ecclesiastical discipline. Like

<hr>

[1] *Inst.*, IV, i, 7.   [2] *Ibid.*, IV, i, 4.

206

his opponents, he believed that there was only one true universal Church. He was far enough from wishing to set free the human spirit from moral and religious tutelage, and the Genevan theocrat would have had all men in an ecclesiastical school far more strict and efficient than that over which the Pope nominally presided. Only Calvin was sure that the papal Church was not the true Church, and its discipline not a discipline in godliness. So far had it departed from the Scriptural norm that it represented Antichrist. " The Papists practice a grosser idolatry [than that of Jeroboam]. . . . We can scarcely assemble with them on a single occasion without polluting ourselves with open idolatry. The principal bond of their communion is certainly the Mass, which we abominate as the greatest sacrilege."[1] The 'note' of the true Church for Calvin is that it is Scriptural, and in the application of this principle he goes farther than either Luther or Zwingli. For him custom and tradition have no authority; nothing must be admitted into the worship and order of the Church which cannot be found in the Bible, wherein alone authority resides.

The ecclesiastical polity which followed from these principles was necessarily marked by two salient features: it was an attempt to reproduce the primitive Christian community as described in the New Testament, and it was not hierarchical. There can be no essential distinction between those who are elect : in the sight of God they are equal. Nevertheless, some are qualified by special gifts for the service of the Church in pastoral offices. Calvin recognises a threefold ministry as warranted by Scripture. The highest category is that of pastor, to which the names bishop and presbyter may also be given. To them is assigned the duty of preaching the Word in the

[1] *Inst.*, IV, ii, 9.

congregation and the administration of the sacraments and discipline. With them are associated elders or lay presbyters, who share in the government of the Church. The third class is that of the deacons, whose office is to care for the poor and sick. This principle of lay representation in the government of the Church is fundamental and is important in its bearing on the political influence of Calvinism. In Geneva, where Calvin's influence was sometimes supreme, he never succeeded in making himself and never wished to become a dictator. The affairs of the Church were carried on by discussion in which laymen took part. But perhaps another feature of Calvin's ecclesiastical organisation was even more important in its political results. He revived the democratic idea of the necessity of popular consent in the appointment of pastors. There is, he holds, " a common right and liberty " in the Church to a voice in the election of ministers. "It is a good remark of Cyprian when he contends ' that it proceeds from divine authority that a priest should be elected publicly in the presence of all the people, and that he should be approved as a worthy and fit person by the public judgment and testimony.' . . . It is a legitimate ministry according to the Word of God, when those who appear suitable persons are appointed with the consent and approbation of the people." [1]

If Calvinism has been one of the nursing mothers of civil liberty it has performed this function by reason of its theology, its moral discipline, and its ecclesiastical organisation, and not because of any conscious effort on the part of its founder to realise a free state. The doctrine of election was a potent tonic to steel the nerves of humble men against the terrors of princes. One who is assured that he is numbered among that eternal aristocracy of

---

[1] *Inst.*, IV, iv, 15.

heaven whose names were determined before the foundation of the world may well feel contempt for the pomp of
kings, who are often only too plainly numbered among the
reprobate; and even though his creed may not encourage
or even countenance rebellion, at the last the fire will kindle,
and he will speak with his tongue—and do more than speak.
The austere discipline of the Calvinist *régime* is the very
antithesis of what the modern world means by liberty, but
it was a preparation for freedom. "The rough education
of Calvin, imposing on his disciples the law of labour and
of moral obligation, revealed the dignity of man and prepared him to deserve freedom." [1] The self-determining
religious communities of the reformed faith were seed-plots
for the democratic state.

Compared with these forces which Calvin released, almost unconsciously, to ferment in the social life of Europe,
his actual opinions and pronouncements on political theory
are unimportant. The fundamental question which has to
be considered is that of the relation between the Church
and the State, and in order to obtain anything approaching
a coherent view from Calvin's writings on this matter it
is useful to distinguish between his conception of an ideal
condition of things and the duties of the Church in circumstances far removed from the ideal. It is commonly asserted
that Calvin was an advocate of a theocratic theory of government and that his theocracy meant the complete subordination
of the civil Government to the ecclesiastical. "Calvin and his
followers taught," says Dr G. P. Gooch, "that the Church
should dominate the State and control the life of its members." [2] This is possibly the logical outcome of Calvin's
position, and his activity at Geneva may not inaccurately
be described as tending toward this goal. But, on the

---

[1] F. de Crue, *L'action politique de Calvin* (Geneva, 1909), p. 6.
[2] *Political Thought in England*, p. 201.

other hand, his formal doctrine appears to be that Church and State are co-ordinate institutions, each of divine authority and each possessing rights in its own sphere. There is in him at least the germ of the thought of a " free Church and a free State." He is utterly opposed to " those infatuated and barbarous men " who wish to overthrow that ordinance of civil rule which has been established by God. Not less does he condemn those " flatterers of princes " who encourage them to extend their power beyond its appointed limits. For these limits may be defined, and the spheres of the ecclesiastical and the civil power respectively marked off from one another. They may be described as the external and the internal. The Church is concerned with the spiritual and eternal interests of man, while the State has the office of caring for his bodily and temporal needs. " He who knows how to distinguish between the body and the soul, between the present and transitory life and the future eternal one, will find no difficulty in understanding that the spiritual kingdom of Christ and civil government are things very different and remote from one another." [1]

Nevertheless, this separation of Church and State is not consistently carried out even in Calvin's theory, and, indeed, we can see very well that any radical distinction between them was not compatible with his most fundamental convictions. There cannot be two final ends, one for the Church and the other for the State. The supreme end and purpose of every institution can be nothing but the glory of God. Hence both civil and ecclesiastical authority should be tending to promote the same end, and there can be no inherent distinction in their purposes. We must also never forget that for Calvin the Will of God was to be found revealed in the Bible with clear finality, and that his

[1] *Inst.*, IV, xx, I.

own interpretation of the Bible was to him the only rational one. Thus the ideal state will be in practice though not in theory a theocracy, based upon a revealed divine law interpreted by ecclesiastics. The city of Geneva, though it never in Calvin's own opinion approximated to his ideal, was regarded by his foreign disciples as the model of what a state might be ; and there we find a nominal distinction between the civil and ecclesiastical polity, combined with a real subservience of the civil power. Indeed, the civil Government appears at times to have been more fanatical than the ministers, for in the case of Servetus the magistrates insisted on burning, in opposition to Calvin, who desired a more merciful form of execution.

In Calvin's theory of the state the magistrates are under obligations of a religious kind. The " maintenance of true religion and virtue," to use the language of the Prayer Book, is their highest duty. They are foolish, says Calvin, who " would wish the magistrates to neglect all thoughts of God, and to confine themselves entirely to the administration of justice among men; as though God appointed governors in His name to decide secular controversies and disregarded what is of far greater importance, the pure worship of Himself according to the rule of His law." [1] Calvin is a firm adherent of that belief which has probably caused more human misery than any other—that it is the duty of governors to enforce religious conformity. Nothing certainly could be farther from his mind than the conception of religious tolerance. " When the Papists are so harsh and so violent in defence of their superstitions that they rage cruelly to shed innocent blood, are not Christian magistrates ashamed to show themselves less ardent in defence of the sure truth ? " [2] The episode of Servetus

---

[1] *Inst.*, IV, xx, 9.
[2] Correspondence, September 9, 1553, quoted by de Crue, *op. cit.*

reminds us that we are not reading a pious opinion remote from actuality, but that what Calvin wrote he was prepared to act upon to the death.

We must turn now to the subject of Governments which are not ideal, and ask what duties have Christian men with respect to them. Calvin's reply to this question, which, we must remember, was one of pressing urgency to many of his disciples, may be summed up in a phrase—passive obedience, with one reservation. He thought that he found in St Paul clear directions on this matter, and he sought no farther. Tyrants no less than governors who perform in a godly manner the duties of their office are raised up by God, the former to be the agents of His wrath as the latter are of His mercy. A man of the worst character who holds sovereign power " ought to be regarded with the same reverence and esteem which they would show to the best of kings." [1]   Moreover, it is not our province to attempt to remedy these evils, which must be accepted as divine chastisements for sin. We may only pray that the heart of the tyrant may be changed, or that God may overrule the wickedness of rebellious men so that, though they add to their own damnation by rebellion, their sin may turn out to the advantage of the oppressed children of God.[2]   " Though the correction of tyrannical dominion is the vengeance of God, we are not therefore to conclude that it is committed to us, who have received no other command than to obey and suffer." " If we have this constantly present to our eyes and impressed upon our hearts, that the most iniquitous kings are placed upon the throne by the same decree by which the authority of all kings is established, those seditious thoughts will never enter our minds, that a king is to be treated according to his merits, and that it is not reasonable for us to be subject

[1] *Inst.*, IV, xx, 26.   [2] *Ibid.*, IV, xx, 30.

to a king who does not on his part perform towards us those duties which his office requires." [1]

The connexion of this political doctrine with the pre-destination theology is sufficiently obvious. We must observe that the Government is to be obeyed not because it is legitimate according to some test which can be applied by the human reason, but simply because it exists. Its legitimacy is implied in its existence, because it could not exist without the Will of God. A distinction therefore appears between the passive obedience enjoined by Calvin and that which became, under the Stuarts, a favourite tenet of Anglican divines. Filmer and his brethren claimed only that we owe obedience to sovereigns who are legitimate according to the patriarchal theory; Calvin invests every *de facto* Government with divine authority, and, save in one particular, would not have been more favourable to resistance than Hobbes. We must observe, however, that Calvin's view is really in fundamental disagreement with that of Hobbes, since he definitely excludes anything in the nature of a social contract. There is, indeed, one minor reservation, of which too much has frequently been made by writers on the history of political ideas. In a few unemphatic sentences Calvin asserts that it is the duty of magistrates who occupy positions in constitutional states to defend the traditional rights of their offices and to fulfil faithfully the charge of protecting the people. But this is no real exception to the general principle, for such magistrates have the same kind of authority as kings. They have come to be where and what they are by the divine ordination: they must fulfil the purpose which has placed them there. The real interest lies not in what Calvin says about the rights of magistrates, but in what he fails to say about the rights of the people. We shall search his writings

[1] *Inst.*, IV, xx, 27.

in vain for any recognition of the principle of democracy or any but contemptuous references to the mass of citizens.

The one serious reservation which Calvin makes in this sweeping doctrine of government is concerned with religion and not with politics. The civil power has no authority in things pertaining to God. Hobbes' view that the subject ought to adopt the religion of the governor would be to him the most horrible blasphemy. If the governor orders us to join in superstitious worship we must disobey. "We ought to obey God rather than men." Even in that case we must not rebel or do anything against the persecuting power. We must suffer anything rather than submit to the impious edicts of modern Jeroboams. "If they command anything against God it ought not to have the least attention, nor in this case ought we to pay any regard to the dignity attached to magistrates."[1]

It is perhaps one of the minor ironies of history that one whose explicit teaching was almost wholly on the side of established authority should have given a powerful impulse to movements toward freedom and democracy. Calvinism in Scotland, Holland, and England was in effect though not in intention a liberating political influence. The causes of this we have already partly seen, and they are in fact not difficult to discover. To some extent they are historical and in a measure inhere in the doctrine itself. The Calvinist congregations found themselves everywhere in opposition. They represented the shock troops of the reforming movement; and it is not easy even for a Calvinist to pray against the wickedness of those in high places while refraining from all overt attempts to bring about the answer to the prayer. It was at least a psychological feat which Calvinism did not succeed in performing. The Churches thus scattered in hostile environments were, moreover,

[1] *Inst.*, IV, xx, 32

of necessity self-governed.   They had to provide for their
inner welfare without the assistance or interference of
authority from outside.   In this way that democratic element in the government of the Church, and particularly
in the appointment of pastors, which Calvin never fully
carried through in Geneva, became a leading characteristic of Calvinism elsewhere; and the habit of democracy
formed in ecclesiastical life could not be restrained in the
long run from affecting political action.   But there is a
deeper cause in the doctrine itself.   It is possible to deduce
two opposite conclusions from a belief in predestination.
It may lead, as it did in Calvin's own mind, to a slavish
theory of the duty of submission.   But another and more
inspiring deduction is possible.   If in the eternal purpose
of God the human race is divided into the elect and the
reprobate, the saints and the lost, it may seem that it is also
His purpose that the saints should rule the earth and that
it is their destiny to overthrow the ungodly rulers.   The
reservation which Calvin made to his doctrine of obedience,
that we must obey God rather than men, cannot easily be
confined, as he confined it, to the question of worship.
It may be that God has commands other than those concerning cult and Church, and that in the State itself the maxim
applies.   If we had to sum up Calvin's influence in a
phrase we could not find a better one than this: he taught
his disciples that we must obey God rather than men.   His
weaknesses arise from the fact that he was too positive that
he knew always what God commanded, but his impressive-
ness comes from this profound conviction, an impressive-
ness which remains although his theology is antiquated and
diluted even in the Churches which call themselves by his
name.   We must obey God rather than men—a message not
perhaps without value even in the politics of to-day.

W. R. MATTHEWS

BIBLIOGRAPHY

A. PRIMARY SOURCES.

CALVIN, JOHN : *In Novum Testamentum Commentarii*, edited by A. Tholuck. Berlin, 1833–4.
    Institutes of the Christian Religion, translated by H. Beveridge. Edinburgh, 1879.
    Opera in *Corpus Reformatorum*, vols. xxix–lxxxvii. Brunswick, 1869–97.

B. SECONDARY SOURCES.

BANKE, HERMANN : *Die Probleme der Theologie Calvins.* Leipzig, 1922.
CRUE, F. DE : *L'action politique de Calvin.* Geneva, 1909.
DOUMERGUE, E. : *Jean Calvin.* 5 vols. Lausanne, 1899–1910.
HUNTER, A. MITCHELL : *The Teaching of Calvin.* Glasgow, 1920.
MENZIES, ALAN : *A Study of Calvin.* London, 1918.
REYBURN, HUGH Y. : *John Calvin.* London, 1904.